Mamma

Mamma

reflections on the food that makes us

MINA HOLLAND

First published in Great Britain in 2017
by Orion Publishing Group Ltd
Carmelite House, 50 Victoria Embankment
London EC4Y 0DZ
An Hachette UK Company

10 9 8 7 6 5 4 3 2 1

Text © Mina Holland 2017
Design and layout © Orion Publishing Group 2017

The author is grateful for the permission to reproduce Rachel Roddy's Pasta
and Potatoes recipe (pages 166–167), first published in *Five Quarters: Recipes
and Notes from a Kitchen in Rome*, by Saltyard Books, an imprint
of Hodder & Stoughton, in 2015

A CIP catalogue record for this book
is available from the British Library.

ISBN: 978 1 4746 0062 0

Illustrations: Loulou Clark

Printed and bound by CPI Group (UK) Ltd, Croydon CR0 4YY

MIX
Paper from
responsible sources
FSC® C104740

www.orionbooks.co.uk

For more delicious recipes, features, videos
and exclusives from Orion's cookery writers,
and to sign up for our 'Recipe of the Week'
email visit **bybookorbycook.co.uk**

For my very own Mamma,
with love and thanks
forever.

Contents

———.———

Introduction

——— . ———

The recipe is a highly-charged autobiographical form.

Nigella Lawson, *Woman's Hour* on Radio 4, October 2015

Not irresistible tastiness but the very failure of food to reward is what drives us to eat more of it. The most sumptuous experience of ingestion is in-between: remembering the last bite and looking forward to the next one.

Lionel Shriver, *Big Brother*

First we eat. Then we do everything else.

M.F.K. Fisher

On my thirtieth birthday, my mum handed me a blue tin box. Lifting the lid, I found inside a stack of indexing cards covered with Mum's scrawl. The top one read 'Mina's Recipe Heritage Box': here was a collection of recipes, all stalwarts from my childhood, each handwritten on its own card – the ingredients and method on one side and, on the other, the story of how that dish had come into my life.

Some had been passed down from previous generations, others Mum had discovered or created herself. But they all had family in common. The recipes were a shared set of culinary foundations, an edible home-turf, almost gene-like in the way they connected us. She'd included Pegasus eggs, the stuffed eggs with anchovies that she'd had as a kid and then served at my eighth birthday party, renaming them after the winged horse of Greek folklore (because everything needed to have an equestrian slant when I was eight). Also masoor dahl, which dated back to her discovery of Madhur Jaffrey when she was pregnant with me, and plum and almond shuttle – the tart fruit encased with frangipane inside puff pastry – a recipe from a book by Steven Wheeler, who Mum had interviewed in the eighties while she worked as a reporter for the Islington Gazette. It's easy, very good, and at the time it was fairly unusual (I still don't really know what a 'shuttle' is) – three things that qualified it for Mum's culinary canon.

Recipes are more than instructions for making a particular dish. They are part of our biographies, living stories, solid, fixed facets of our past, and adaptable, always developing, features of the present and future. Like people, they change. Some of the meals I grew up with are like characters to me, old friends that have taken on lives of their own and evolved over time. I'm much more interested in a recipe when I understand where it has come from and the story behind it. As an editor, it is wonderful to see a renewed interest in home cooking, which in turn generates great appetite for recipes. But publishing them without a delicious preamble that explains their significance to the contributor – their inspiration, how they might have been altered, any memories attached to them, and so on – often leaves me a bit cold. How many salads or curries or trifles can you edit before they start to blur into one? What I do know is that when stories accompany recipes, they stand out; stories make me want (or not want, as the case may be) to cook them; stories mean a recipe and its creator are more easily archived in my mind, ready to pull out and make again when I see fit. Simply, if my imagination is inspired by what has been written about a dish, I will be more inclined to bring that dish to life.

This was really the spirit in which we launched our residency column in the *Guardian Cook*, the supplement I co-edit, back in 2014. We wanted to give emerging cooks a temporary platform to share their stories, with three pages to fill with an article, two or three recipes and tips, every week for a month. More often than not, these pieces revolve around family, and are always inspired by memories. There's Olia Hercules, Ukrainian chef and author of *Mamushka*, who each week took a different one of her four grandparents' eastern European nationalities and wrote of how each shaped her cooking. And Rosie Birkett, whose first column happened to go live on the tenth anniversary of her father's death. She marked the day by including a recipe for home-made salad cream in homage to his insatiable penchant for it flung all over a pile of lettuce and peas he'd grown in his garden. Meera Sodha – whose Gujarati grandparents came to Lincolnshire in the UK via Uganda – negotiated these three influences and produced platefuls that delighted and surprised, like Lincolnshire sausage curry. In every case, the recipes would have meant little had their heritage, or the story of their inception, not been explained.

'We stir readers when we add food because we remind them of their places at the complicated buffet of self, family, culture. Our recipes are histories of who we are, transmitting the tastes of the past through precept and example, even as they suggest how we can sometimes revise our lives by adjusting the menu', says Sandra M. Gilbert in *The Culinary Imagination*. Gilbert's book is a scholarly work on food and cultural identity, but I think its title alone harmonises with what I'm getting at: that cooking and eating are as much an imaginative act as they are physical and functional. Lionel Shriver's quote at the beginning of this introduction ('The most sumptuous experience of ingestion is in-between . . .') nods to the same thing: that the anticipation of food is a more delightful experience than its acquisition, or that the idea of food when hungry trumps that same hunger being sated. The stories behind recipes are crucial to how good they taste. Fantasising about food, or food imagined, or all the invisible and intangible stuff that comes alongside a dish that you're really craving is, I think, key to why you crave it so much.

In 'Hunger Games', an article she wrote for the *Guardian* in early 2016, food writer Bee Wilson said: 'Our tastes follow us around like a comforting shadow. They seem to tell us who we are.' Though not impossible to change, Wilson explains how children learn their tastes, habits, even idiosyncrasies surrounding food in early infancy; a person's identity around food, in other words, is established at a very young age. Our food habits when we are two, she says, are a pretty accurate gauge of how we will eat when we are twenty. And it is because these habits are emotionally loaded – it's *comforting* to gorge on sweets, or *disappointing* if you don't clean your plate, or *naughty* to play with food, and so on – that they become harder to shift in adulthood: 'We make frequent attempts – more or less half-hearted – to change what we eat, but almost no effort to change how we feel about food . . . .'

So food isn't just food. It's emotional, it's imaginative and it identifies us. And I am far from being alone in finding this interesting. There are now magazines, podcasts and even a Netflix series dedicated to the human stories behind what we eat. Where in mainstream newspaper publishing, the *Cook* residency is unusual in the space it affords cooks to write about their recipes, the online world indulges a growing demand for food narratives and confessionals. Take the *Lucky Peach* magazine, which in 2015 launched a 'Mom Month', showcasing interviews with working (chef) mothers including Alex Raij and Margot Henderson, features about mother-child cooking (most notably Alice Waters and her daughter Fanny Singer on her favourite homecoming dish – an egg cooked in a spoon over a fire), and a piece by the magazine's chef creator, David Chang, on his two grandmothers, whose respective cookery skills sat at opposite ends of the talent spectrum.

The rising popularity of informal restaurants suggests that the gap between home cooking and fine dining might be closing. Informality is no longer a symptom of the 'cheap eatery', but an aspirational feature of the high-end restaurant. Customers can share a table with strangers, their food served on communal platters, perhaps on mismatched crockery, while garnishes, menus in French, sommeliers talking in what seems like code suddenly seem out of fashion. I think people feel further removed from good, home-cooked food; their regular workhorse, weeknight meals aren't the hearty platefuls their mum might have prepared, but more likely something picked up from a supermarket convenience-food aisle on the way home. Having comforting, nutritious food cooked from scratch, then, is more of a novelty that it once was; we can't take 'mamma's cooking' for granted.

There is a particularly striking example of this in London – a food business-meets-social enterprise called Mazi Mas. Set up by Greek-American postgraduate Niki Kopcke, Mazi Mas – which in Greek means 'together' – sets out to put migrant and refugee women into work in a UK kitchen. This comes in the form of a 'roaming restaurant', which has just found itself permanent premises in Hackney, east London. Each night, the culinary theme reflects the woman heading up the kitchen – Roberta from Brazil, maybe, Azeb from Ethiopia, or Zohreh from Iran – not only introducing British palates to the home-cooked food of their home country but, importantly, demonstrating that restaurant food needn't be the work of trained chefs. Plates of *moqueca de peixe* (Brazilian coconut fish stew), *gheymeh bademjan* (yellow split pea stew with saffron and aubergine from Iran) and spreads of Ethiopian *wat* stews and *injera* pancakes emerge from the kitchen and offer diners an insight not just into those cuisines, but into homes too.

Another social enterprise, also in London, has set out to use the universal medium of food as a conduit to group therapy. Natale Rudland Wood's 'Recipes for Life' methodology was inspired by a period working in a juvenile detention centre, and the 'very different sorts of conversation [that] seemed to be possible in the kitchen . . . as recipes unfolded so did people's stories'. Food memories acted as a talking point through which to access the patients' emotional worlds, and the familiar vocabulary of cooking, used allegorically, provided a framework for healing. The group talked about ingredients (for example, 'hope', 'perseverance', 'irrational optimism', maybe even 'prayer'); sourcing, to locate those ingredients ('family history', 'spiritual beliefs', 'folk culture'); recipe method ('combine honesty and patience, include a dash of desperation'), and serving suggestions ('family support', 'grandmother's presence'). The group then presented their recipes for life with one another, over an actual meal. Here food provided the opportunity to talk both physically, over the dining table, and metaphorically as well. It is on the subject of technique that I found Wood's idea most poignant; she said, 'sometimes techniques are the result of a mistake . . . in life very important knowledge comes from our mishaps . . . this is true in the world of cooking too'. More of this in the 'Improvisation' chapter.

Whether its associations for you are positive or not, food is endowed with personal and cultural meaning for *everyone*, and what we eat is often inextricably plaited into our emotional state, hence ideas around 'comfort eating' to self-soothe (even if that eating eventually makes our stomachs feel quite *un*comfortable). It is usually via parents that we experience nourishment for the first time. They introduce us to food, teach us about how to eat it, when to eat it, how to interact with it . . . And, more often than not, it is our mothers – the original nurturers, if we are lucky to have ours in our lives – who are responsible for making those early food memories and for establishing our tastes. So, the story starts at home. Yes, we grow up and become independent eaters with the agency to choose what food we will and won't eat, but those early meals – the ones you had time and again, the ones that smell and taste like home – remain with you forever.

If they have good associations for you, they'll still be there waiting for you to fall back on them.

In my case, they're in a blue tin box.

✳ ✳ ✳

Mamma is the title of this book in homage to where everyone's food story starts: the mother. But *Mamma* is also a reference to home cooking, to 'mamma's cooking', the food that this book champions. It is perhaps an unusual format for a food book – neither a straightforward recipe collection nor a piece of food writing in the conventional sense, but, rather, an assemblage of interviews, anecdotes, recipes and notes, all of which reflect on this idea that the food we eat (and cook) is integral to who we are. It is an exploration of food as a clue to identity – a process that begins in infancy, possibly even in the womb.

I believe this to be a universal truth. Every time the theme of this book comes up in conversation, people eagerly share with me their own food memories and talk about dishes their mum made them. People love to convert other people's perceptions of a dish they grew up with – a lasagne, perhaps – from being just another lasagne to a lasagne with profound and ineffable meaning. We all know the stereotypical Italian who says their *nonna* makes the best ragu/meatballs/risotto/whatever, and this is my case in point. As US food writer Bill Buford wrote in *The New York Times*, 'One of the great charismas of food is that it's about cultures and grandmothers and death and art and self-expression and family and society – and at the same time, it's just dinner.' Food is (or should be) mundane – we all need it, we all eat it – and yet, when the casserole is made by your mum, or when the cake reminds you of an absent friend, or when the lettuce was grown nearby, or when you've visited the bakery where the bread was made, it becomes personal, and that endows it with a kind of magic.

Here I have profiled eight figureheads in the food industry, each with a unique attitude to food. Though they don't all necessarily chime – Claudia Roden is a stickler for tradition, for example, while Yotam Ottolenghi believes a cook should feel empowered to toy with conventions – they all agree that childhood is a vital and formative time for establishing our eating habits. With these interviews, I wanted to bring those individuals to life, show something of them, their lives, their histories, their beliefs and how they eat by painting a written portrait of the time I spent talking to them. We start with their childhoods, usually with a focus on their mothers – as Jamie

Oliver said to me, 'it all starts with the boob' – and look at how food has shaped their lives. Stanley Tucci tells of what cooking has taught him about creativity. Never having learned to cook as a girl, Anna Del Conte only started out of necessity when she got married and moved from Italy to England ('a sad story in the 1950s, when it came to food'). Alice Waters' mission is to get children gardening and to give them a holistic understanding of where food comes from, which will lead to a better diet by proxy. Jamie Oliver's campaign is to address childhood obesity with measures such as a sugar tax; and psychotherapist Susie Orbach is less worried about *what* people are eating and more concerned about *why* they developed 'anguished' eating habits in the first place. These are just a few examples of the themes that crop up herein.

In addition to these eight profiles are eight chapters, each with a theme that pertains to food and what it says about our identity: such as nature, tradition, improvisation, women, balance, togetherness, obsession and meat-eating. I've had fun writing these; they've been an opportunity to tell some of my own food stories, which, I hope, raise some universal and relatable truths.

Then there are the ingredient sections – eight in total – that cover all the fundamental tenets of my home cookery: eggs, seasoning, potatoes, pasta, yoghurt, vegetables, pulses, and spices and herbs. These are the ingredients that I grew up with *and* which form what Jamie Oliver described as the regular 'palette' of my kitchen, the workhorses of my fridge and cupboards. All are affordable, and all – with the exception of the vegetables – are perennially available, with a view to giving you recipes you could, like me, make all year round.

More than this, though, I've chosen to write about ingredients that I believe have made an indelible mark on me. Eggs were the beginning – my early meals – and, well, everything starts with an egg, doesn't it? (Don't tell the chicken.) By attuning me to ideas around balance and my own palate, seasoning made me more self-aware. Over potatoes I have forged relationships and made lasting friends. Pasta made me want to learn how to cook, and has kept me cooking. Yoghurt has tempered both my recipes and my childish rages. Vegetables made me discerning. Pulses made me tick along, forming the backbone of my diet, an essential, thrifty, comforting source of protein. Herbs and spices make me experiment, daring myself to try making things a little differently, each and every time. (And leftovers made me resourceful.) This is almost my family tree of ingredients: they have made me who I am today. You will have your own equivalents.

Following these notes are recipes that put the ingredient in question to work. It has been said that mothers rotate nine recipes to feed their families so how, you might ask, is it possible for me to have so many more go-tos in my collection? The simple answer is that everything I make is a variation on a few themes – the different yoghurt dips are a good example – all riffs on a similar idea with a few basic flavours changed here and there. Lots of my recipes were born by accident, created out of leftovers from a previous dish. Home cooks are masters of reinvention, one meal seamlessly running into another: the vegetable boiling water becomes a kind of stock, the oil from the braised vegetables forms the basis for a pasta sauce, the leftover pasta makes a tortilla. In essence, there are straightforward ways of adding variety to home-cooked food without changing the basic things that you buy.

Some of the recipes here are dishes I grew up with, real home staples of my childhood that now live on in my adult life, some

I have invented, and some I have learned from others, built on myself, and adopted into my own canon of things I like to cook regularly . . . This is a book as much about how food becomes a part of our lives – the roles and guises it assumes – as it is about the direct relationship between parenting and food. So all of the recipes have a story, and all are things that I regularly throw together, ranging from the prosaic to the altogether odd.

For the most part, though, my recipes aren't wacky. In fact, they're often quite bland. Blandness comforts. People are often surprised by the plainness of the things I favour eating: pasta pomodoro, a baked potato, wilted spinach with lemon juice, dahl and rice, braised lentils and kedgeree. Wholesome and very often rooted in my past, this is the food I come back to, time and again. Most of the time, I crave ordinary goodness in what I eat at home. (This was certainly the case when I returned to my mum's house while writing this, heavy with flu. The first food I had eaten in two days was a Quorn lasagne, which I think most chefs would have called under-salted if they'd got so far as trying it . . . I realise the word 'Quorn' can be a barrier to entry! In any case, it hit the spot, in fact it was the only thing I wanted.) Contrary to what the publishers of restaurant cook-books might think, I don't think most people want to eat like they're in a restaurant at home.

The majority of my recipes haven't been written down before now. It'll become clear in the 'Improvisation' chapter that I don't follow recipes very often at home, unless I'm doing something technical like baking, playing with oil and fat (i.e. deep-frying), or trying to recreate something very particular (Moro's chicken fattee – I'm thinking of you). With food, I prefer guidelines to rules. One of the reasons I've always been reticent about writing recipes down is that I prefer to cook intuitively and never make something the same way twice. The specificity of recipes, the pressure to follow them to the letter, can stunt creativity. So make the recipes in this book your own, treat them as ideas, starting points, rough formulae – the quantities of ingredients or any additions/exclusions are your call. So many of the recipes in these pages hardly qualify as such; where I give you a description rather than a list of ingredients and a method, I hope you feel unpatronised rather than short-changed. This passing down – inheritance, if you like – is entirely natural, and it is how food evolves. For this reason, I don't believe in culinary plagiarism; derivation is inevitable in cooking – we pick things up along the way, absorbing them into ourselves so that their genes change yet live on. Like the people that make them, all recipes have a genealogy.

These days it's very easy to romanticise food. Those working in food media, as I do, are particularly susceptible to a blinkered outlook on the modern foodscape. Judging by my email inbox, it's all artisan produce, natural wine bars and pop-up restaurants, with much less heed paid to the rising demand for food banks, or to animal welfare standards in the meat industry. A recent article on www.firstwefeast.com points to some of the shortfalls in the food media, one of which is this overt over-emphasis on positive reporting; it seems we are poor at covering the less palatable side of this industry, preferring to leave that to politics and opinion channels. The other day I was talking to a colleague about a rather lacklustre piece that a particular contributor had filed. It was full of rich imagery from their childhood feasts, with dazzling descriptions of dishes and family rituals. Yet still it bored us. 'It's nostalgia', said my colleague, 'there's just too much food nostalgia out there.' I nodded in agreement, quietly anxious that this book might contribute to that tidal wave of food nostalgia. Yes, my own food memories – some sublime, some ridiculous – play a role in these pages, but rather than rose-tinting my life in victuals, I hope to have shown honestly how food has shaped me and the subjects I have interviewed, much as it will have done you too.

When we met, Susie Orbach said something that really struck me. She talked about the importance of parents cooking with their kids 'to make food very ordinary as well as extraordinary'. Food is both normal and awesome, and it is perhaps on accepting this duality that we can have a healthy relationship not just with food itself, but with ourselves as well.

Negotiating
tradition

——— . ———

Tradition is important to me because I saw how much it mattered to all the stateless Egyptian Jews who, like my family, found themselves in London . . . it made them feel they belonged to something bigger.

Claudia Roden, interviewed in London, July 2015

Without tradition, art is a flock of sheep without a shepherd. Without innovation, it is a corpse.

Winston Churchill

Granny's vinaigrette went something like this: four tablespoons of olive oil, three tablespoons of wine vinegar, a loaded teaspoon of Colman's mustard powder, two crushed garlic cloves, salt and pepper. Together, we would ritually measure these components out, then shake them up in a jam jar before slapping the thick liquid over bright green lettuce sitting expectantly in the wooden bowl.

After we'd eaten the salad, with whatever else was on that evening's menu, the acid sting of raw garlic and rough vinegar would sit in my stomach and repeat . . . and repeat. Still, I insisted that my grandmother's was the only vinaigrette that would do. I remember giving my mum a hard time for putting balsamic, or lemon, or a little sugar into her salad dressings, seeing any deviance from the way Granny did it as an act of heresy. Her way was gospel. It's taken me until now to admit that – with the benefit of hindsight, and having made many salad dressings in my time – I've had better.

With food, tradition is an evangelical presence, guiding everything from its creation to how we congregate around it; from ingredients and techniques right through to when we eat and how, what and who we do it with. This is obviously true from a cultural perspective. Food is integral to how people live together and how communities evolve. As the Claudia Roden quote earlier suggests, food evokes in us a sense of belonging to something – to a place, or to a group of people. It identifies.

It struck me that the same can be said of our attachments to 'family cuisine'. If part of food's magic is Proustian – about memory – then it's hardly surprising that we become attached to the way it was originally made for us, how it first tasted. Food vividly recalls the intangible past, channelling the person who made it, those we ate it with, and wherever we were as we did so. Family traditions can be as strong, sometimes stronger, than broader cultural ones.

I have spent a lot of time thinking about this question of tradition with regard to food. My first book, *The Edible Atlas*, set out to break down a set of culinary traditions into simple, digestible building blocks, helping people to acquaint themselves with said cuisine at home. It was no mean feat, for three reasons:

1. Culinary traditions are vast. The whole undertaking was almost unfathomably huge. A bonkers undertaking, perhaps.

2. Covering a 'cuisine' loosely sums up the general 'rules' of a national or cultural cuisine, but it doesn't take into account the idea of family cuisine, which I touch on earlier.

3. Cuisines change all the time. As people move around, particularly with the march of globalisation, the whole world becomes a melting pot of ingredients, cultures and families that cross-pollinate. Writing a book like *The Edible Atlas* could only ever be a generalised snapshot of the moment it was written in time.

For these reasons, tradition in cooking can be problematic for the enthusiastic cook. It can cause an identity crisis. How do we negotiate the rules that we grew up with? How do we honour those culinary roots without compromising on creativity? How do we become 'our own cook' in the shadow of the parental ones from whence we came, and to whom we have become attached?

After my granny died in 2004, I tried making her salad dressing for a while, but it was never the same without that deep, dark wooden bowl, without the verdant Norfolk lettuce awaiting the ochre slop, without her there to swipe every last drop out of the jam jar, and to sit opposite me as I ate it, chewing in her one-sided way (she'd had a brain tumour in middle-age that had left half her face paralysed). In the end, I stopped making it. I went to university, never had powdered mustard in the house, and developed a mild intolerance to raw garlic (disaster). It was liberating to start using lemon juice, some honey, *wholegrain* mustard; to accept that adhering to Granny's recipe wasn't going to bring her back. To borrow Woody Allen's words, 'tradition is the illusion of permanence', and my religious devotion to her mediocre vinaigrette wasn't going to keep her alive. She was gone, but I still had salad to eat and enjoy.

Nonetheless, you can keep someone's memory alive, and I'd argue that food is one of the better mediums for this. Like any food worth making, it just has to taste good. There are plenty of Granny's recipes that I *do* still make, many are peppered throughout this book. Through them, I acknowledge her influence on my cooking, sometimes changing a thing here or there to make them my own. There is huge satisfaction in thinking that I will one day feed my own children meals that my dad, and then my brother and I, were brought up on, knowing that Granny remains the source.

* * *

Arguably, it's impossible to create anything wholly new. Some of the best things are derivative because they are informed, honed versions of something similar but different that came before. Maybe I wouldn't have written this book without other writers who inspired me – Laurie Colwin, Nigella Lawson, Joan Didion. The same could be said of most things ever created – plagiarism it is not, evolution it is. This includes cooking. Jane Grigson acknowledges this in *English Food*:

> *No cookery belongs exclusively to its country, or its region. Cooks borrow – and always have borrowed – and adapt through the centuries . . . What each individual country does do is to give all the elements, borrowed or otherwise, something of a national character.*

Our cooking should be influenced by tradition, but not be beholden to it. Though his cooking is light years apart from my own, the Italian chef Massimo Bottura is insightful on this matter. The menu at his restaurant in Modena, Italy – Osteria Francescana – pays homage to classical Italian dishes and to his upbringing in food, deconstructing the likes of mortadella sandwiches (what peanut butter and jelly is to American kids, this is to the Romagnan child) and reshaping them. The edible result is an act of love *and* subversion. Arguably, this is more of an intellectual exercise than an everyday eating experience – his book, *Never Trust a Skinny Italian Chef,* includes no recipes for his dishes, but a short essay about each (think mortadella mousse with a toasted square of Modenese flatbread laced with lard). Nevertheless, Bottura's emphasis is on – to borrow the zeitgeist's favourite buzzword – mindfulness, when using tradition: 'It is hard to stay one step ahead of nostalgia, but it is important to find that critical distance, to keep moving forward, even when you are looking back.' The point, as I see it, is that the better informed you are about tradition – whether cultural or familial – the better the results if you tamper with it. Perhaps tradition needs to be understood before it is played with? This would help avoid traditions being forgotten and dying.

Clearly, this is a question of balance. Let Jane Grigson give you the nod to borrow from your forebears, and take inspiration from Winston Churchill (quoted earlier) by keeping the guiding light of tradition in balance with your own creativity. By building on what has come before, we are keeping it alive, and cuisine remains a living thing. And, still missing my grandmother and feeling dreadfully guilty for calling her salad dressing mediocre, that comes as a great comfort.

An aside on my Britishness

The modern British cook could be forgiven for feeling rootless. We are, of course, not, for what are roast beef and Yorkshire puddings, Lancashire hotpot and fish and chips if not edible roots? And that's before even mentioning our plethora of puddings, cakes and teatime fancies. But rootless we feel, distanced from and ignorant to a rich and varied culinary history, which in only a century has dulled in our collective awareness.

The likes of Jane Grigson's *English Food* are too monochrome and picture-free to hold much appeal outside of a small readership of food enthusiasts. On a brighter note, Fergus Henderson's *Nose to Tail Eating* was recently[*] voted the best cookbook of all time in 1000 Cookbooks (as voted by food writers and chefs). True to Claudia Roden's point that only innovation is fashionable, digging to the root of any traditional cuisine doesn't hold much mass market appeal in these days of pasta made from courgette and stock rebranded into 'bone broth'. Tradition is a pursuit left to the nerdy.

As a Brit, I've sometimes felt a bit sad that we don't take greater pride in a regional product or dish, like you find in just about any Mediterranean township. I've had to teach myself to make the British classics, just as I've taught myself to cook anything else. How I envy the French for growing up knowing intuitively what wine to drink with which dish, and the Genovese for the pesto that virtually seeps from their pores at birth, and the Puglians' deftness at making orecchiette (you get the idea ...). It is disappointing that British culinary traditions have been derailed.

[*] In October 2015.

That said, I *do* think there is something to be gained for a cook who has grown up outside of a strong, healthy culinary tradition. A certain freedom, perhaps, from the shackles of *this is how it must be done.* If I want to shove a lime instead of a lemon inside my roast chicken, I will. Likewise if I feel it's better (and more inclusive) to roast potatoes with good olive oil rather than duck fat – which I always do.

Claudia Roden

Claudia Roden is wringing her hands. 'There's a Turkish-Jewish dish that's a bit like spanakopita, but with milk – it's called *boghatcha* – a filo pie with three cheeses, that's then drowned in the milk. It's fantastic. I *could* do it with pumpkin, lots of herbs, preserved lemon . . . but would that make it any better?'

Claudia's editor has asked her to enter new territory. She may have dedicated her career to unfurling the home cooking of different Mediterranean cuisines, but this is uncharted land of a different sort. She has been asked to write a book, which, rather than pursuing the traditional food of a region (with authentic recipes), puts new spin on those she has already written about – with a particular emphasis on ease and simplicity.

But Claudia doesn't like cutting corners. She strikes me as walking precision. She speaks slowly, with meticulous enunciation, a hint, perhaps, at her almost religious approach to doing things properly. 'Deconstructing old dishes is popular among young chefs now . . . but I don't know why you'd deconstruct an old dish if it's already good. You don't go on cooking something, generation after generation, if it isn't good. That's why I feel tradition is valuable.'

I'll admit, the layers of filo pastry, pumpkin, preserved lemon and so forth all drowned in milk had sounded pretty tempting,

and I was rooting for Claudia to get cracking on the recipe, but she had a point. Why deviate from a traditional recipe if it already tastes delicious?

In 1956, Egypt's Jews were given two weeks to leave the country and Claudia's parents came from Cairo to join her in London, where she was an art student at the time. For her (delighted, I'm sure) peers at St Martin's, Claudia would sometimes prepare the staple meals with which she'd grown up – hummus, kibbeh (lamb meatballs) – but it was only when her parents arrived, and they experienced sudden, collective statelessness, that she began to cook in a big way. For refugees, she says, food is integral to surviving both physically *and* emotionally – a touchstone of home.

Her parents always hosted Friday night Shabbat dinner in Golders Green and her mother, never much of a cook before, would make Jewish family comfort food of the sort that had seldom left Egyptian home kitchens – things like chicken sofrito, where the bird is cooked with garlic, lemon, cardamom, turmeric and chickpeas. In this fragile climate, food offered tangible comfort. People would come over for dinner and leave saying, 'I might never see you again, please give me the recipe for your chicken sofrito [or whatever dish it was].'

'I never once saw a cookbook in Egypt', says Roden, 'and recipes weren't written down. In fact, people guarded their recipes jealously in Cairo, because if your home cuisine was good, it gave you an edge over others.' Jewish food had always been, she says, a 'secret', both an 'archaic mosaic' and 'just home-cooking'. But in London, recipe sharing became a community duty, and learning to cook Jewish home food well, with limited resources, became a project for Roden's mother – and one to which Claudia has remained devoted ever since, collecting recipes obsessively. They went to Mrs Harrel's Cypriot shop in Camden for the (then rare) aubergines and courgettes they needed to make *dolma*, to Kentish Town for the filo pastry to put together *knaffeh*, to Indian shops for tamarind. Some things they couldn't find – chickpeas, couscous – and others, like pomegranate molasses, they learned to substitute with lemon and sugar. For Claudia, a passion for cooking was borne from necessity, as was the practice of using food as a lens to look at cultures, including their own threatened one. 'Through recipes, a culture can be understood. Food became my way of uncovering the past', Roden says.

Put this way, it's easy to see why Roden has been so uncompromising about adhering to tradition, and why her (impossibly glamorous) eighty-year-old hands are being wrung at the thought of tampering with *boghatcha*. This dish's name alone points to a rich history: a Judeo-Spanish interpretation of the Castillian word for 'drunkard' (*borracha*), and the three cheeses (feta, Gruyère, Parmesan) *and* butter *and* milk reflect the preponderance of dairy-only meals that Turkey's Sephardic Jews often kept separate from their meat-based encounters. Seen like this, food *can* educate us about the past. She describes how she gasped on discovering a reference to Treya, a 13th century Jewish recipe for pasta with apricots, in the British Library's only Arab cookbook, a dish that her aunt Regine had made in Aleppo. Until she arbitrarily fell upon it that day in the library, she hadn't seen it since she was a child. She also talks about how the *conversos* – the Spanish Jews who converted to Christianity in the late 15th century – made puff pastry with butter and pork fat, demonstrating to the inquisitors with the latter that they had, truly, converted. All are ways of tracing the complex, and often hidden, legacy of Jewish food.

Roden remembers being invited to speak at a conference on Egyptian food in a Cairo hotel some years ago. The event posed the question: 'What is Egyptian food?', the subtext being – for an audience of hoteliers and restaurant managers – 'What *should* we be serving?' After her initial reaction ('You threw me and my people out of the country when I was seventeen and now *I'm* invited to tell *you* what to eat?!'), she decided to go. Years of badly parroting French nouvelle cuisine had left Egyptian restaurants with an identity crisis, and with something of a schism between head chefs brought in from overseas, and their local, more lowly, kitchen staff who, she says, were ashamed of their mothers' cooking. This she set out to tackle, recommending they reintroduce a 'heavenly' green leaf stew that descends from the pharaohs called *melokheya* – but taking care to use the particular aromatics (like cumin, coriander and garlic) that mark Egyptian cooking apart from its Turkish and Cypriot counterparts* – as well as stuffed pigeon, and vegetable and rice dishes like koshari.

When asked for her opinion on food, she will always recommend that a place stay true to its roots. She despairs about a world in which food is so global and industrialised that all variety is lost: 'Fashion is boring. Who wants to have the same food everywhere they go? You want to experience the people, the landscape, the architecture, that distinguish groups of people from one another.' She goes on, 'I don't think cuisine stands still: society changes, people move. But it changes slowly. It's the self-conscious, overworked innovations that chefs are under pressure to make that bothers me.' She's referring to the

---

* Where *melokheya* also exists, but where the spicing changes in favour of cinnamon and allspice.

likes of one Egyptian chef trying to serve her a mash-up of local and *nouvelle* cuisines – think *ful medames* (Egyptian fava beans cooked in garlic, onion and lemon) in choux pastry, or a tabbouleh with mussels, even a pastilla with Indian chutney. You start to see why 'fusion' became a dirty word to many chefs in the nineties and noughties.

For Roden, culinary innovation isn't by definition bad, but it should be done with consideration. Food indicates belonging to something bigger than yourself and your immediate surroundings, and what you eat is an identity. 'I find now that when I meet people from Egypt, we are brought together by our food memories. It's an intimate thing, sharing the same background in eating. There's an instant bond there, a humour.' Culinary tradition is a window to understanding and connecting with another person.

Could it be, then, that tradition has a parental role for Claudia Roden? I think so. She finds it hard to talk about her mother's food without referencing the whole community of Jewish Egyptians in London in the fifties. I don't think that is to deny her mother's importance, but more to celebrate her in grander terms. As I picked at almond cake in her kitchen – all Arabesque tiles, family pictures, her own oil paintings – it dawned on me that family and the food cooked in the Jewish tradition are near-inextricable for Claudia. True to the words of French historian, Fernande Braudel, who Claudia quotes herself, 'the smell of cooking conjures up a whole civilisation.'

I told Roden not to be frightened of playing with her *boghatcha* recipe, and indeed, I'm hoping her new version with pumpkin and preserved lemons does come to life. After we met, I received an email from Claudia which elaborated on her upbringing in food. I've left the paragraphs below as she wrote them, because they read like poetry.

> *Going shopping with my mother and helping with the cooking that she put so much passion into created a very special bond between us. My parents lived a few minutes walk away from me in Golders Green. I would speak to my mother every day and visited them often. The smells from their kitchen made me feel we had never left Cairo. My brothers and their families and my own family never missed a Friday night dinner or a festive meal at their house. When my younger brother died suddenly in his late forties my mother was so grief stricken she could not carry on with these and I took over at my house.*
>
> *When I was collecting recipes for the Jewish book I was sometimes given some unnecessarily laborious recipes that weren't even very good and were particularly unhealthy by our standards. The women who gave them usually said that when their mother died they took it upon themselves to cook their mothers' recipes for the family. For them dishes were also about identity and continuity and remembering generations past.*
>
> *Eating round a table whether you are two or fifteen does create a bond as does working together in kitchens.*

Eggs

— ✁ —

It was known as the white seat. A big, fitted bench that lined one wall of the kitchen, which had a PVC cover that wiped clean. My lasting memory is its surface – glossy, shiny – like the white of a boiled egg after the shell has been carefully peeled from its flesh. That was when it was clean, which, I'll be honest, wasn't often.

And that was the thing about the white seat – it showed everything. Ketchup smears and over-zealous squeezes of chocolate sauce; spilt juice, with clothing fibres dried onto it; paint; felt tip pen; beaten eggs that slid keenly from the bowl in which they'd been beaten – a little strayed and the whole lot followed. It was disgusting and we loved it.

The white seat and eggs collided more than a few times during my childhood. It's where my early cooking took place, the supervised cracking of eggs into batter for some half-hearted beating and some whole-hearted bowl-licking once the mixture was ready to bake. But I think it was the intolerance to messing up that the white seat and eggs really had in common. Both ruthlessly unforgiving, the white seat punished the house-proud parent, while eggs for the cook are a tell-tale sign of your (in)competence. The perfectly oozing orange globe within a boiled white; a poached egg with a white that's compact and coherent (not the ethereal, watery fragments that so easily emerge); scrambled eggs with chunky yellow curds ... Getting eggs right, *au point,* can be a question of seconds – and getting them wrong is just so easy.

During the year in which this book was written, I spent a lot of time thinking, talking and writing about eggs. I helped to develop a restaurant menu dedicated entirely to them. *Guardian Cook* produced a supplement all about cooking with eggs. I lived in a vegetarian home and, as such, cooked a lot of eggs myself too. Eggs offer the cook endless possibilities, but somehow – for every eggs Rothko, or carbonara with pork belly, or rum and raisin soufflé recipe that cropped up – nothing seemed to compare to eggs in their plainest forms. Like people, eggs need only be themselves to be their honest best.

Jane Grigson said, 'egg dishes should be nothing if not a combination of simplicity, purity, flavour and richness.' On all this she is right, I think, except for the richness, because I often turn to eggs when my appetite is in flight from heavy food.

There are, of course, many rich and fabulous ways with eggs, like the Burgundian speciality *oeufs en meurette* (eggs poached in a thick sauce of red wine, bacon, onions and burnt butter), and many of these are as delicious as they are photogenic. But get to grips with the basics of egg cooking – the poaching, the frying, the scrambling and the boiling – and you have the power to make yourself the simplest of meals *and* the wherewithal to spruce up a too-basic plateful. Eggs need little more than a drizzle of olive oil or some tomato sauce to find their summit of goodness. I often see them as the way to improve an existing meal, a way of lifting even the most insubstantial-seeming ingredients: wilted spinach with a fried egg or a poached one atop a mound of vegetables; hard-boiled eggs chopped up over some steamed leeks and vinaigrette, fried ones roughly cut up and tossed into spaghetti with olive oil and cheese, even a single egg baked into the cavity of an avocado with a smear of harissa.

Nail eggs and the world is your oyster . . . or just a world of better-cooked eggs. Quo Vadis' head chef Jeremy Lee gave some very useful advice on the holy grail of egg basics (from the fittingly titled *Guardian Cook* 'The Egg Bible' in 2015), which I've paraphrased below:

1. Fried eggs – it's hard to screw up a fried egg, just make sure you fry it in olive oil rather than butter; butter burns and turns the egg's edges brown. If you don't like a bubbly and crispy white (I don't) make sure the heat isn't too high.

2. Boiled eggs – a regular-sized egg needs only 5 minutes of a rollicking boil to have a set white and soft yolk. Drop the egg in once the water is boiling.

3. Scrambled eggs – the opposite of fried eggs, these guys love butter. Grease the pan with butter and add in seasoned beaten eggs (Jeremy includes cream, another friend uses mascarpone, both are rather wonderful . . .). I can't bear scrambled eggs that are too fine, almost grainy. You want what Jeremy calls 'large curds', achieved by stirring the eggs 'in a slow figure-of-eight manoeuvre'.

4. Poached eggs – I've messed up so many poached eggs in my time and can conclude the trick is not to panic when making them. Simply have your pan of water at a gentle simmer and add a teaspoon of vinegar, which will help the egg whites coagulate – i.e. stop them from disintegrating in the water (annoyingly, this *will* affect the taste of the egg . . .). Break

the egg into a teacup and then, with a spoon, create a whirl-pool in the simmering water – the momentum this creates will prove essential in keeping the egg together. Drop the egg into said whirlpool and leave to poach for 3–4 minutes, after which you remove the egg with a slotted spoon.

Always buy the best eggs you can: large, free-range, organic if possible. Well might you roll your eyes at this, but while the difference in price isn't huge, it is in quality. In *More Home Cooking*, Laurie Colwin says it is a fact that how a chicken has been reared impacts emphatically on how good its eggs taste: 'There is no question about what makes a good egg . . . [one] from a free running chicken has a high, plump yolk . . . and taste[s] intensely . . . like eggs: nutty, buttery, chickeny.' It follows that less-stressed chickens produce better eggs (I'm sure the same is true of humans). Eggs are the most basic of ingredients, and also some of the most precious. Do them proud.

PEGASUS EGGS

These are the stuffed eggs from a horse-themed birthday party my parents once threw for me. The name – which was in homage to the winged stallion that carried Poseidon, Greek god of the sea (not that I had any idea of this aged 8) – has stuck in my family, but on reflection I realise it's pretty apt: the eggs are a noble white vessel for a heavenly load, paradoxically better known as devilled eggs.

For about a year I co-ran a supper club called The Novel Diner (a pop-up for hungry readers); we would each month choose a different novel on which to theme a meal, and for The Great Gatsby *we served another version of these eggs as canapés and called them 'East*

and West Eggs' – a nod to the two Long Island spits of land (East
Egg and West Egg) separated by a bay in the novel. We used bite-
size quail's eggs, mixing red paprika into the filling for East Eggs
(to represent the red light that shines across the bay to West Egg) and
finely chopped parsley in with the West. The recipe below is for the
equestrian version from my childhood.

———

SERVES 4–8

4 eggs

2 anchovy fillets

1 tbsp mayonnaise

black pepper, to taste

pimentón or pul biber chilli, to serve (optional)

———

1. Hard boil the eggs by putting them in a saucepan of cold water, then
   placing the pan over a medium–high heat. Bring to the boil and cook
   at a rapid simmer for 5 minutes before turning off the heat and
   leaving the eggs in the pan of water for a further 5 minutes.

2. Meanwhile, blitz the anchovy fillets in a processor, or chop them up
   very finely. Mix in a bowl with the mayonnaise and black pepper.

3. Drop the cooked eggs into cold water. When they are cool enough
   to handle, peel and halve them, removing the hard yolks and
   mixing them into the mayonnaise and anchovy mixture.

4. Place a spoonful of the mixture into each hollowed-out egg half and
   serve with a sprinkling of pimentón or pul biber chilli on each one.

Where eggs really excel is the all-day breakfast. In my house, the four dishes below are usually late morning, weekend affairs, but they all make a complete meal at any time of day.

BAKED EGGS

I suppose this is a take on Israeli (or, more accurately, originally Egyptian) shakshuka, but I've bastardised it so much that I wouldn't make any claims to authenticity. So 'baked eggs' it is, rather less pleasingly rhythmic than its Middle Eastern alter ego. I could, and do, eat this at any time of day and am convinced it would convert even the greatest cynics (my mother) to tomato sauce at breakfast. If you prefer, leave out the sage and rocket and keep it plain. Alternatively, I suggest adding half a teaspoon of dried chilli flakes and half a teaspoon of pimentón to the sauce.

———

SERVES 2–4

6 tbsp extra virgin olive oil

2 onions, sliced into half moons

1 tsp ground cinnamon

½ lemon, for squeezing

3 garlic cloves, finely sliced

1 heaped tsp harissa, or to taste

2 x 400g tins of good quality whole tomatoes, drained

2 tsp tomato purée

8 sage leaves

70g (or 1 bag) rocket

4 eggs (free-range and organic, if possible)

sea salt and black pepper

To serve

3 tbsp natural yoghurt

sourdough, toasted

———

1. Heat 3 tablespoons of the oil in a large, deep sauté pan (as wide
    as a 30cm frying pan) over a low–medium heat. Add the onions,
    a sprinkle of the cinnamon and a squeeze of lemon juice, and
    sauté for 10 minutes.

2. Add the garlic and cook for a further 3 minutes, then add the
    harissa. Cook for a minute or so, then tip in the tomatoes and
    break them up to create a chopped tomato sauce consistency.
    Add the tomato purée, 3 of the sage leaves, most of the remaining
    cinnamon, another 2 tablespoons of the olive oil and season well.
    Leave to simmer for 15 minutes.

3. Heat a drop of oil in a small frying pan over a medium heat
    and add the remaining sage leaves left whole. After a minute or so,
    add the rocket and wilt it down, sprinkling in a touch of salt as you
    go. Remove from heat and set to one side.

4. Taste the sauce and adjust the seasoning to taste (or perhaps you'd
    like more spice, in which case add a touch more harissa). Some of
    the water from the tomatoes will have evaporated and you'll be
    able to form 4 little wells in the sauce, which almost hold. Quickly

crack in the eggs. Sprinkle a little sea salt and grind some pepper onto each, half cover the pan and leave to simmer. Now is the time to use your instinct; you want the egg white just to have turned from clear to white – time this well and you'll still have beautiful runny egg yolks.

5. Remove the eggs in sauce from the heat, then distribute the wilted rocket over them. Place the whole sage leaves on top too, in a pretty formation. Dollop the yoghurt on top, drizzle with the remaining olive oil, grind over some pepper, sprinkle over the remaining cinnamon and serve immediately, with sourdough toast.

EGGS IN
AVOCADO CRADLES

I first made this when I had a proliferation of avocados and a particularly bad hangover. No, I didn't want to go and buy tinned tomatoes for baked eggs, and no, I didn't want to wait long for anything to cook. We had several avocados and eggs and on switched a light bulb. The egg inside the avocado makes this cooking at its most photogenic.

———

SERVES 2–4

2 ripe avocados

4 tsp harissa

4 eggs

salt and black pepper

To serve

extra virgin olive oil, for drizzling

pimentón (optional)

sourdough, toasted

wilted spinach (optional)

———

1. Preheat the oven to 200°C/400°F/Gas mark 6.

2. Halve the avocados and remove the stones but leave the skins on. Arrange the avocado halves cut side up on a small baking tray – I find a loaf tin is a good size for holding them in place.

3. Smear 1 teaspoon of harissa into the cavity of each avocado half, crack the eggs into a bowl and then scoop up the yolks 1 by 1, accompanied by some of the white, with a spoon and drop them into the cavity.

4. Sprinkle with salt, grind over some pepper and place in the oven. Bake for about 15 minutes, until the egg is cooked and the yolk is still partially runny. The cooking time will depend on the size of your avocados and the quantity of egg.

5. Remove from the oven, drizzle with extra virgin olive oil and dust with pimentón, if using, then serve with sourdough toast and some wilted spinach, if you like.

LEFTOVER PASTA TORTILLA

I live with a tortilla enthusiast — a tortilla obsessive, even. I like this alternative to the classic potato version because it doesn't rely on the meticulous potato prep and deep-frying that tortilla Española demands. I often have quite a bit of leftover pasta and, for the purposes of this recipe, am all for it sticking together (stuck together spaghetti does a great job of binding the tortilla into a fabulous starchy, eggy round of goodness that looks like Pacman when you take out the first slice). If there's sauce on the pasta — there usually is — then so much the better. This recipe uses the spaghetti left over from cooking for a crowd (i.e. there's quite a bit remaining!).

———

SERVES 4

8 eggs

75g Parmesan, grated

extra virgin olive oil

2 garlic cloves, minced

450g leftover pasta

salt and black pepper

———

1. Beat the eggs in a large bowl with the grated Parmesan, 1 tablespoon of olive oil and the garlic, and season with salt and pepper.

2. Add the pasta to the bowl and mix thoroughly, so that it's completely coated in the egg mix.

3. Put a small non-stick frying pan over a high heat and leave it for a couple of minutes to get very hot, then add 1 tablespoon of oil. This should start to 'melt' into the pan after a minute or so, at which point you can add the egg and pasta mix. Evenly distribute it across the pan, then reduce the heat to medium.

4. Cook for around 5 minutes, or until the pasta tortilla starts to pull away from the sides of the pan. Cover with a plate, then flip the tortilla onto it.

5. Return the pan to the heat, add a little more oil, then slide the tortilla back in, cooked side up. Cook for a further 5 minutes, then serve.

EGGS IN CELERIAC MASH

This came into being because I was left with a mound of cold, very salty celeriac mash after having people over. It was so salty, in fact, that it needed to be calmed down by something plain. Potatoes came to the rescue, then eggs swooped in and elevated it into a complete meal. I've since discovered that Fergus Henderson does something similar without the potato; he also uses celery leaves and butter instead of olive oil. It's a dish you can play around with. I'm sure it would be great with wilted garlicky greens or some cooked-down leeks mixed in. The quantities here are based on the weight of celeriac I had left over (roughly 500g), so adapt the quantities to what you have. The recipe doesn't rely on leftovers, instead taking the celeriac from raw.

———

750g potatoes, peeled and cubed

500g celeriac, peeled and cubed

5 tbsp extra virgin olive oil

80g pecorino cheese, grated (optional)

6 eggs

parsley or chives, chopped, to serve (optional)

seasoned yoghurt (page 230), to serve (optional)

salt and black pepper

———

1. Preheat the oven to 200°C/400°F/Gas mark 6. Cook the potatoes and celeriac in 2 separate pans of generously salted boiling water, until soft enough to yield to a masher. Drain.

2. Transfer the cooked potato and celeriac to a bowl and mash together, add 4 tablespoons of the olive oil, season with salt and pepper and, if you want to include it, add the cheese.

3. Put the mash into a large ovenproof dish, and make 6 little wells in the mixture to welcome each of the eggs. Crack them in and grind some pepper on top.

4. Place the dish in the oven and cook until the whites are solid and the yolks still molten. Remove, drizzle with the remaining tablespoon of oil and serve. Sprinkle over the chopped herbs or serve with the seasoned yoghurt. It's especially good with the seasoned yoghurt.

I f the tortilla and baked eggs recipes weren't enough proof of the ongoing love affair between eggs and onions, here are two more recipes to showcase it . . . Two very different, equally ultimate, examples of their sweet, golden and unctuous union.

CHARRED RED ONIONS VINAIGRETTE

Like much of my cooking, this was born out of laziness. I wanted something quick, and I didn't want to go shopping. I had a lot of onions, garlic and some eggs.

I have a soft spot for a stalwart of a British dish, leeks vinaigrette – that delicious symphony of allium, hard-boiled egg and a dressing rich in mustard – which I think is a meal all on its own with just a piece of bread. I recreated it using red onions – another allium, after all – and it worked a treat. Their charred sweetness (and the accompanying griddled bread, if you decide on that) is a bit reminiscent of Turkish mangal grills.

SERVES 2–4

4 red onions

4 tbsp extra virgin olive oil

2 tbsp red wine vinegar

1 tbsp Dijon mustard

4 eggs

celery leaves or chives, to serve

bread, for griddling (optional)

salt and black pepper

———

1. Prick each onion a couple of times with a fork or skewer, then
   rest the onions over an open flame (you could also put them high
   up under the grill, but I like what direct contact with the flame
   does to the flavour of the things). Cook them for 15–20 minutes
   depending on the size of the flame (as big as possible). Turn the
   onions with tongs to make sure they blacken all over: you want
   them so black that little flakes of burnt skin fly around the place
   like amaretti biscuit wrappers, and the interior feels soft and
   yielding. Remove from the flame and leave to cool a little.

2. While the onions are cooling, quickly make the vinaigrette.
   Whisk together the oil, vinegar and mustard with a tiny dash
   of cold water, season with salt and pepper and set aside.

3. Put the eggs in a pan of cold water and place over a medium heat.
   Bring to the boil and then simmer for 5 minutes before turning off
   the heat. Leave them to sit in the water for a minute or so. Drain,
   fill the pan with cold water and set aside.

4. Peel the onions and cut them into pieces – I like to keep the length
   of the whole onion and for the width of each piece to be about
   1cm wide. It doesn't matter too much if a few charred flecks make
   their way onto the plate, but try to avoid it if possible.

5. Dress the onions with the vinaigrette (you may not need it all) then
   set to work peeling and chopping the eggs finely. My mother likes
   to cut the whites up very small and then push the yolks through
   a sieve – this looks very pretty if you can be bothered. Scatter the

chopped eggs over the dressed onions and top the plateful with
a grind of black pepper and the celery leaves and/or chives (I like
both). If you have griddled some good bread, and have olive oil
to accompany it, so much the better.

EGG, ONION AND COCONUT CURRY

*This curry is divisive, mainly because I love serving the eggs with
runny yolks, and not everyone's a fan of a runny yolk. If you want
to serve it my way, you'll need lots of yoghurt naan bread (pages
241–242) and rice to soak up the liquid.*

—

SERVES 4–6

3 onions, 1 halved, 2 sliced into half moons

4 garlic cloves

4cm piece of fresh root ginger

3 tbsp solid coconut oil (or vegetable oil)

1 heaped tsp ground turmeric

1 heaped tsp garam masala

½ tsp ground cardamom

½ tsp chilli powder

1 tsp salt

1 tsp sugar

1 tbsp tomato purée

3 tbsp desiccated coconut

200ml warm water, plus an extra splash

6 eggs

½ lemon, to serve

plain rice, to serve

naan, to serve

yoghurt, to serve

———

1. Blitz the halved onion, garlic and ginger in a blender until they form a paste. Heat 2 tablespoons of the coconut oil in a frying pan over a medium heat, add the paste and fry, stirring frequently, until its eye-watering rawness dwindles and it starts to take on colour.

2. Mix the spices, salt and sugar together in a bowl, then add this mixture to the paste along with the onions and the remaining tablespoon of coconut oil. Coat the onions in the spice and paste mixture and cook, stirring, for about 2 minutes.

3. Add the tomato purée, desiccated coconut and warm water to the pan. Bring the mixture to the boil, then simmer for 5 minutes before turning off the heat. Cover the pan and set aside until the eggs are ready.

4. Put the eggs in a pan of cold water and place over a medium heat. Bring to the boil. They should be on the hob for 10 minutes (if you prefer them hard-boiled, make it 15 minutes). Once this time is up, plunge the eggs into cold water and peel. Drop the peeled eggs into the curry pan and coat them all in the glossy, orange-brown sauce. Place the pan back over a medium heat, cover and simmer for 2 minutes.

5. To serve, cut each of the eggs in half to reveal a molten centre. Squeeze a little lemon over the top and devour with plain rice, naan and yoghurt.

I tend to stay away from anything technical in the kitchen, leaving the likes of soufflés to those better prepared and less haphazard than myself. I usually rule out recipes that involve separating yolks from whites because the half that isn't called for usually languishes in the fridge for a week, only to be thrown away. As a Hispanophile with a weakness for custard, I couldn't exclude *crema Catalana* – that Catalan confluence of egg yolks, milk, citrus, vanilla and cinnamon, left to set in ramekins – from this chapter, but I also couldn't include it without making some suggestions for putting your egg whites to work: the part which both binds and billows, and the secret behind so many light desserts.

CREMA CATALANA

—

SERVES 4–6

150g white sugar (granulated or caster), plus extra for sprinkling

4 egg yolks

1 cinnamon stick

1 tsp vanilla bean paste or 1 vanilla pod, split lengthways, and seeds scraped out

grated zest of 1 unwaxed lemon

2 tbsp cornflour

240ml whole milk

———

1. Beat the sugar and egg yolks together in a bowl until fluffy and almost forming a foam.

2. Add the cinnamon, vanilla paste or seeds and lemon zest then sift in the cornflour. Transfer the mixture to a saucepan and pour over the milk.

3. Place the saucepan over a low heat and cook the mixture gently for about 10 minutes, stirring constantly, until it thickens and reaches the consistency of custard.

4. Decant the mixture into ramekins or Duralex glasses and leave to cool at room temperature, with a little sheet of greaseproof paper over the top of each to prevent a skin forming, then transfer to the fridge.

5. If you are making crema Catalana, sprinkle about 1 tablespoon of sugar over the top of each ramekin or glass, so that there is an even layer covering the crema's surface, then use a blowtorch (or the grill) to create a burnished sugar crust. Or, if you want to make the Catalan mess below, leave as they are.

CATALAN MESS

New takes on the Eton mess — that glorious splat of meringue, cream, summer fruit and mint — are not uncommon. But, shortly after the disastrous results of the EU referendum, I decided there had been quite enough Eton messes for, well, a lifetime — even the delicious kind. So I used the egg whites left over from a crema Catalana to make this, a 'Catalan mess', a reactionary, and more left wing, answer to an otherwise Tory pudding! Were you to make it really Catalan, you might also add some poached quince and crushed toasted hazelnuts. But it works with just about any fruit, nut, herb or spice. A little saffron water drizzled over the top would give orange opulence, or some ground cinnamon perhaps. I love it with any berry, some thyme, nutmeg. Make it your own.

———

SERVES 6

1 quantity of crema Catalana (see pages 45–46)

your choice of fruit, nuts, herbs and spices

For the meringue

4 egg whites, at room temperature
(left over from the crema Catalana)

200g caster sugar

———

1. Preheat the oven to 120°C/250°F/Gas mark ½ and line a baking tray with baking parchment.

2. To make the meringue, place the egg whites in a spotlessly clean bowl (or the bowl of a stand mixer) and whisk until fluffy, then start adding the sugar, 1 tablespoon at a time. Keep whisking until the mixture forms stiff peaks, then, with a metal tablespoon, dollop them onto the baking tray, leaving a few centimetres in between each.

3. Place the baking tray in the oven and cook for about 1 hour, or just over, then turn off the heat and leave to cool slowly in the oven.

4. Dollop a few tablespoons of crema Catalana into 6 bowls, sprinkle with crumbled up meringue, then scatter with fruit, nuts, herbs and spices of your choice.

CHILLI AND LIME
COCONUT MACAROONS

These are based on the inspired recipe in Claire Ptak's The Violet
Bakery Cookbook. *The chilli and lime do a delicious job of
distracting you from all that sugar.*

———

MAKES 10–25 MACAROONS, DEPENDING ON SIZE

4 egg whites

250g caster sugar

¼ tsp fine sea salt

1 tbsp good quality honey

200g unsweetened, desiccated coconut

1 tsp cayenne pepper

zest of 2 limes

———

1. Preheat the oven to 180°C/350°F/Gas mark 4 and line a baking tray
   with parchment.

2. Simply put all the ingredients into a saucepan and place over a
   low–medium heat. Stir continuously, making sure the ingredients
   are evenly distributed. The mixture will seem very dry, but will
   loosen as the sugar dissolves. Keep stirring until it starts to thicken
   but take care it doesn't stick – until, as Claire says, it takes on the
   consistency of rice pudding.

3. I like to make mini macaroons using a heaped teaspoon –
   you could also do bigger ones – up to you. Either way, scoop
   individual mounds of mixture onto the lined baking tray, and

leave a little space in between each so that they can expand. Bake in the oven for 10–18 minutes, depending on size, or until the macaroons have become golden and puffed. Cool completely on the baking tray – they will keep for up to a week in an airtight container.

PLUM AND ALMOND SHUTTLE

Lastly, eggs play a supporting but essential role in the sweet dish that most says home to me. I can't think of a better way to end this chapter than to quite literally shuttle you off into pastry ecstasies . . .

My mum has made this so many times that the recipe has become a distant memory. It's best with tart plums to contrast with the sweet frangipane but if your plums are sweeter, or if you fancy making it with different ingredients – as I once did, swapping plums for cherries, and almonds for coconut and thyme – then you'll need to adjust the sugar according to the sweetness of the fruit. Serve with crème fraiche or vanilla ice cream when hot, or revel in it cold at breakfast time.

———

SERVES 6

225g puff pastry

225g plums, halved and stones removed

1 egg, beaten, to glaze

1 tbsp caster sugar

For the almond frangipane

50g softened butter

4 tbsp caster sugar

1 egg, beaten

50g ground almonds

1 tsp almond essence

———

1. Preheat the oven to 200°C/400°F/Gas mark 6.

2. Roll out the puff pastry onto a baking sheet and cut vents diagonally across 1 half of it (so that, when the pastry rises, the plum and almond filling pokes through).

3. To make the frangipane, cream the butter and sugar together in a bowl, then beat in the egg, ground almonds and almond essence until fully combined.

4. Spread about three-quarters of the frangipane mixture across the uncut side of the pastry, leaving a 2cm border untouched. Arrange the plums on top, most cut-side down, but with a couple cut side up, then splatter the plums with the remaining quarter of the frangipane mix, and fold the cut side of the pastry over. Press down the sides of the folded pastry with a fork to secure the edges, then brush all over with beaten egg and sprinkle with the sugar.

5. Transfer to the oven and cook for 45 minutes. The pastry should have risen and the slats should reveal teasing purple bubbles where the softened plums and crispy, exposed bits of frangipane collaborate. Hubba hubba.

Improvisation

———·———

He [Thelonious Monk] played each note as though astonished by the previous one, as though every touch of his fingers on the keyboard was correcting an error and this touch in turn became an error to be corrected and so the tune never quite ended up the way it was meant to.

Geoff Dyer, *But Beautiful: A Book About Jazz*

My mom's cooking is an alchemy. After a while you're in a fucking Kafka play.

Stanley Tucci, interviewed in London, July 2015

Sometimes I think about home cooking like jazz. It sits somewhere between the spontaneous and the controlled. I love the idea of producing food with the same unplanned fluidity of a Miles Davis or a Thelonious Monk. Geoff Dyer's portrait of Monk at the keyboard above, which celebrates the beauty in the haphazard, could easily be superimposed onto a home cook in their kitchen. They never quite know how a dish will turn out, weaving glitches (like missing ingredients) and leftovers into the end result. It makes for a very delicious chaos, one that sometimes doesn't work but, very often, just does. This kind of cobbling together by trial and error, however slapdash it might seem, is a learned art but – whether playing music or cooking –

it takes confidence. For many who cook out of necessity, the jump from following sheet music to jamming is a daunting and bold leap.

Recipes seem to have colonised the world of cooking, but are only one part of the story. They teach you to follow a formula for a particular dish, but only time spent in the kitchen, practise and watching those who do it well can cultivate the sensory approach of the jazz musician.

In the *Guardian*'s weekly *Cook* supplement, our content is governed by the seasons and we experience an annual recipe cycle. Each year, we must both reinvent the season and harness all that is familiar and evocative about it. While there is doubt-less great comfort to be found in cooking seasonally – the summery scent of mint boiling with new potatoes, or the aroma of peel, sweet spice and booze before Christmas – for anyone working on a recipe-led food publication, the test is always to reproduce traditional themes in a novel way.

The year goes something like this: It's January and everyone's on a health kick – anyone for kale? Oranges? Ancient grains? Then there's the hunger gap, when there is no fresh seasonal produce, so it becomes all about cooking from tins. Oh, and look, it's Easter! Chocolate! Eggs! Summer is barbecues and rosé, September means back-to-school lunch ideas, pumpkin pumpkin pumpkin in October and then, well, Christmas. How not to dry-out your turkey. The Ultimate Roast Potatoes, people! 'Interesting sides'. Home-made edible gifts. What to do with your leftovers.

This formula must be quite like the annual curriculum for a teacher: the baseline of information remains the same, even if the characters change. There'll always be one kid at the back of the class sniggering at Goneril's name in King

Lear (I was one of them), or a contributor keen to wax lyrical about blood oranges in January, as though it has never been done before. Nonetheless, like sex, recipes for these things sell. They offer instant gratification for cookery enthusiasts (sumptuous pictures, a precise and immediate formula for 'the perfect coq au vin' or '10 essential ideas with avocado'), while longer-form food features – the stories and contexts for those recipes and, perhaps, the information that really stays with you – have a slower, gentler appeal, demanding more time from the reader.

Perhaps the reason I like the jazz musician analogy for home cooking so much is that it gives doing what might be 'the wrong thing' a green light. In other words, it suggests that nothing is ever wrong when you cook: everything you do is simply an expression of yourself at a certain moment in the kitchen. Cooking is about feeding ourselves, yes, but it is also about understanding your skills, your limitations, your particular tastes. It's about steering the course of things according to what you have in your cupboards and fridge. It's about trying a little of that pickled god-knows-what that your friend brought back from holiday because you're intrigued by it. It's about getting to know what, for your palate, 'a pinch of salt' or 'glug of wine' means. It's about happy accidents and learning from disasters. It's about realising that almost everything tastes better with extra virgin olive oil.*

---

* Though this book is full of recipes – confusing, perhaps, given all I have just written – each one is designed for you to tinker with. These are recipes with which you are free to play. They are my best attempt at recording the previously unrecorded and writing down the formulae for dishes that, until now, have really only existed in my head. They don't seek to spoon-feed, but simply to guide, by handing you a knife and fork and sending you forth to make them your own. Butcher them to your heart's delight.

The director Mike Leigh, cinema's king of improvisation, said of film-making what I would say about making a good home-cooked meal: '. . . it's not all about characters, relationships and themes, it's also about place and the poetry of place. It's about the spirit of what you find, the accidents of what you stumble across.' Each meal has its own character and is unique, from the ingredients you cook with, to the people who are present to enjoy it. There's no recipe for negotiating this randomness, and I think the lesson is just to try things out, giving little deviations from your recipe a whirl. Like Thelonious Monk at the keyboard, it might not end up the way it was meant to, but it could still be a beautiful thing.

A note on leftovers

I tend to build meals around what I have, not what I haven't. I decide what to cook based on what's in the house, or what took my fancy in the greengrocer as I walked home, or – most importantly – what I need to use up. Home cooking is powered by leftovers.

Throughout my life, the remains of the day have informed tomorrow's menu in a kind of culinary relay race. Tonight's pasta meal (of which I will have cooked too much) will run into tomorrow, when another few things – a little butter, some egg – might join with it to form a frittata. This then, in turn, feeds and runs on, perhaps into yet another day: cold frittata with yoghurt and salad maybe, or fried up into a hash. It is this kind of constant reshaping of ingredients that makes home cooking a living flow, marking it apart from the polish of restaurant food or the homogeneity of packaged goods.

Using up leftovers is essentially an act of recycling, traditionally more out of necessity than choice. It makes economic sense, after all, to get full use out of the food you buy. The importance of using up yesterday's food has been hammered into me since I was a kid. Both my parents – two products of four people who had lived through rationing – had been raised to make do, eking out as much as possible from what was sometimes very little.

My grandmother loathed waste, which was informed by her Scottish Calvinist upbringing. 'Waste not, want not,' was order of the day, every day. Granny insisted on clean plates and consciences – throwing food away was almost heretical and she was an expert at making it go further: tired garden veg like carrots, parsnips, radishes, would be grated into a salad, a sort of coleslaw without the mayonnaise, which she christened 'Silflay' (in homage to *Watership Down*, in which it means the act of grazing in Lapine rabbit-speak); dahl would be 'brought back to life' for days after the original batch had been made by adding water and butter; a risotto was just another way to use up leftover sausages and vegetables with the addition of rice. Food was bought or grown to feed the family, down to its last dregs.

All this rubbed off onto my dad indelibly, and now onto me. It has been interesting to write this and witness a familial domino effect of horror at wasting food. This has only hit me as a grown-up; I didn't always share Dad's approach to cooking. My dad is an anti-gourmet food lover – he likes volume and he likes value – and it has taken me until now not to feel irritated by it. I used to envy the Alphabite chips and Angel Delight my friends ate at home while resenting Dad's policy of 'hoovering up' everything from crusty baked beans to twice-baked jacket potato skins, which he'd fry up with butter and bacon and sometimes eggs into some sort of hash or brownish omelette. It seemed singularly unglamorous.

But speaking to him about Granny (my food hero) made the link between mother and son clear to see. Dad's food isn't fantastic by anyone's standards, but knowing it has been made with my grandmother's values makes it – sometimes, only sometimes – exactly what I want to eat. 'Waste is one of the most offensive things for me. I also don't think good food should have to cost a lot, which it seems to nowadays. There remains huge value in knowing how to use ingredients resourcefully, using up every last scrap, which my mother instilled in me.' His culinary philosophy, base as it once seemed, has been inherited from a pro, though it has undergone some unfortunate mutations.

I can't bring myself to throw still edible food away simply because the fridge has wilted it, or because we ate it yesterday and the gloss of freshness has given way to a day-old density. The joy that is bubble and squeak would not exist without leftovers. Fishcakes, using residual mashed potato, would be scarcer, as would the likes of arancini from remaining risotto, countless frittatas and pasta bakes, and any number of puddings involving soaked sponge, like trifle, that put weary cakes to good use. The list goes on. Best of all: cooking with leftovers is a kind of gamble. It can open doors to food you never knew existed.

I spoke to chef Margot Henderson about leftovers and she immediately referenced her husband Fergus, painting a picture of him in bed early in the morning on holiday. He wonders what to do with yesterday's leftovers for lunch ("'What's for fucking lunch?" has ruled our marriage!'). For their family, cooking with leftovers – whether in risotto bakes, using up cold meats, stale breads, or in frittatas – comes hand-in-hand with a lot of fat and white flour. She's got a point – on the fat front, anyway – and it took me back to my granny. She had an uncontrollable penchant for butter, which seems to explain so much about her ability to make anything taste good.

Leftovers are enhanced versions of their predecessors then, in no small part because they require more imagination (and butter). I posted a picture of my second day lentils on Instagram (witness a 21st century 'old-fashioned cookbook' which makes up for its picturelessness with references to social media), on which the Italian food writer Eleonora Galasso commented: 'There's something unmistakably honest about eating leftovers, maybe because the cook's good intentions have been put into their ingredients for a second time around, and most eloquently.'

Stanley Tucci

When I visit the Tucci residence in west London, it is everything you want it to be when you walk into an Italian-American household.* There are beautiful teenagers with huge Disney eyes, almost cartoon miniatures of Tucci himself, casually wandering in to open the enormous fridge door (a door bigger than one of them) and gaze at its contents. There are numerous copper pans dangling on one side of a stove and, on the other, ancient menus that Stanley has collected from antiques shops over the years. There's an alcove brimming with culinary volumes and a tempting rack of Piemontese bottles that I eye up. When I ask for some water, I'm instructed to help myself and, looking for a glass, open a cupboard stacked from floor to ceiling with cans of San Marzano tomatoes . . . It is a lovely, proper, lived-in home, full of people who love to cook and eat.

As I bask in these excellent first impressions, I have no idea that the best is yet to come. A woman with glasses and dark, short-cropped hair pads into the room and nonchalantly greets me. We are introduced. Mina, this is Stanley's mother, Joan. Ladies and gentleman, there's a mamma in the kitchen. I've

---

* Not least the home of the star and director of *Big Night*, the 1996 film about two Italian brothers who run a failing Italian restaurant on the New Jersey shore. It's a movie in which food is holy ('to eat good food is to be close to God') and eating is a conduit to happiness ('bite your teeth into the ass of life').

come to interview Stanley Tucci about food and his mother, and on arrival The Woman Herself emerges *and asks me if I want to eat arancini with her.* I must say I'm pleased.

So, Joan casually offers me rice balls from a shrimp and pea risotto (pronounced *riz-oh-toh*) that she made two nights ago. I obviously accept, watching as she drops oil into her sauté pan and deftly swirls it about the surface with her finger. I make conversation and she is direct, not chatty, and very likeable. I sense her interest in me is mildly piqued by questions about her rice ball frying technique. A plate is passed over and the now spherical risotto has acquired a golden crust. I bite in, and it tastes of home. Not my own home, but a home I could spend a lot of time eating in.

When Stanley and I talk – post-arancini, and over espresso – the daily emphasis he places on food becomes quickly clear. He tells me that he avoids working on films that involve a lot of night shoots because they prevent him making an occasion out of dinner. He says few things make him sadder than room service. No no, he likes to return to his trailer and make a Martini, scrub up, put on a jacket and go out for a meal – even if he's alone – at a restaurant in whichever small town he might be near, which he will have researched. He makes this effort for food.

There has been no great discovery of good food for Stanley Tucci because good food has been bred into him. He grew up in New York State, but both sides of his family are Italian and, as a child, they would visit either set of grandparents every other Sunday. These visits would revolve around the meal.*

---

* This seems to be the difference, for Stanley, between food now and how he grew up to appreciate it. Food for him is everything, not an accessory or lifestyle choice. 'Eating and cooking have become adjunct to human life, not integral to it,' he says, railing against the words with a hit of coffee after speaking them.

He remembers going to friends' houses and eating Velveeta cheese in the 1960s ('a rectangular block, supposedly like Cheddar, but kind of Cheddar fused with uranium . . . what Spam is to meat, this was to cheese') and realising just how good his mother's cooking was. A home-cooked meal might consist of pasta with marinara sauce, or veal cutlets with a vegetable side, perhaps green beans, or broccoli di rapa, or a tomato salad – it would depend on the season. That said, he tells me his mother is practically vegetarian, existing on a diet of mostly pasta, potatoes and beans. 'Meat is the difference between Italian and Italian-American food,' he says. Tucci's family are from Calabria where inferior meat, limited funds and dazzlingly good vegetables combine to create a cuisine in which meat is either a bonus or an afterthought. But when Italians came to America, they had access to meat in abundance for the first time. They really made sure they made the most of it (meat-feast pizza, anyone?).

Tucci's grandfather could grow anything. Stanley remembers picking string beans from his garden, which Joan would magic into a *minestra*,* along with zucchini, garlic and fresh tomatoes. To this day, when Tucci's own string beans and zucchini are in season in London, he'll make this practically every day. This is the dish that takes him home. Likewise, the smell of a freshly grown carrot will transport him to his grandfather's garden. A light Orvieto wine, the kind that almost looks like water, reminds him of holidays with his late wife, Kate. Cucumber

* A *minestra* is generally considered to be a first course in an Italian meal, though for the poor, it would traditionally have been the dish around which a whole meal revolved. Administered as it would have been from a central pot, its name derives from the verb 'to administer'. It is a thick soup or stew, usually with some kind of carbohydrate component – pasta, rice, potatoes – combined with intensely flavoured stock and often pulses.

salad with a little vinegar, olive oil and oregano of summer suppers with his now-wife, Felicity: 'these are my emotional anchors, my edible triggers.'

Joan Tucci has no interest in baking. When I ask Stanley if she ever cooks from a recipe, he answers yes, 'but she'll instantly augment it, because she knows what she likes so well.' He recalls rallying the troops to test recipes for his cookbook, *The Tucci Table*. A gifted cook, Joan was, obviously, included in those troops, 'but was impossible to pin down on measurements: she never knew how much of anything she used, and constantly revised what she'd said before.' Tucci impersonates his mother resentfully shrugging her shoulders at all this emphasis on cups and, worse, the metric system. And then he likens her cooking to the obscure brilliance of a Kafka play and I nod, because he probably couldn't have put it better. There *is* something immeasurable about good cooking, and the great cook's prowess might always be shrouded in mystery.

'It's like acting too, you just have an instinct that you could do what the director says, but your instinct makes you feel it when it's wrong. So much of what I do as an actor is instinctual, and I guess that's how Mom cooks. For me, cooking is an opportunity to use my instincts elsewhere. I inherited a palette of ingredients and a desire to eat from my family, then I had to teach myself to use those things . . .'

Stanley then says that all he wants to do is cook, because it teaches him about the creative process and, he's realised, all the same rules apply to every artistic endeavour.

Stanley Tucci's rules that apply to every creative process

1. Less is more. No one can teach you that. You need to go through it yourself to find out. (Southern Italian food was borne out of necessity and is a reminder that all you really need is fire and water to cook, which makes cooking from scratch easier nowadays because we have boiling water and we have stoves.)

2. It's all subjective. There'll be some people who love what you make, and others who don't.

3. Ultimately, you have to keep doing it because you love it. (Stanley loves to cook outside in pits of fire with loads of cast iron and rustic stuff. He likes Tom Kerridge's chicken with hay. Sometimes it works perfectly, other times it's a disaster. Even if the product is terrible, he has enjoyed the process.)

4. You have to go beyond what's comfortable.

'Why do I care about food? Because it's all there is. It keeps us alive and connects us to one another . . .' It is almost as though he realises how important food is to him as he speaks the words. 'Food and cooking connect you to everything. To every part of society, from the ground up. Who grows the food? Who reaped it, processed it, delivered it, butchered it? And once all that's done, it connects you to the people you love when you share in it. It's *that* connectivity. It's the creativity. It's sharing it with other people . . . It's very hard for me to connect to people who don't care about food.'

Pasta

I can only hope that my boyfriend will live up to Pasta in the long run. If in him I have found humanity's answer to this most loyal of foodstuffs, I will be one lucky woman. Pasta has been a constant in my life: comforting, supportive, reliable . . . and it keeps on surprising. We have a very happy relationship.

I loved it from the moment we met – probably some limp fusilli with grated Cheddar and ketchup on a Beatrix Potter plate – and my feelings have only become stronger as the years have passed. My pasta memories exist in vignettes:

a) Eating red-sauce-soaked spaghetti and sucking it through my lips so that bloody flecks showered my cheeks. I was particularly fixated on the scene in *The Lady and the Tramp* in which the two dogs accidentally share a piece of spaghetti and their snouts meet in the centre. I desperately tried to convince my friends to recreate the scene with me. I don't think I ever succeeded.

b) The greatest treat was going to tea at a particular friend's house because her mother would make penne with béchamel, tuna, sweetcorn and cheese. So good. I won't have a word said against it (although it was invariably followed by strawberry Angel Delight, which I am probably less inclined to defend now).

c) Friday nights in with Petra, my one-time-au-pair-and-now-Czech-sister, when we'd watch *Friends* on a beanbag eating a Lloyd Grossman sauce with a tin of tuna over macaroni.

d) Cooking noodles with tinned tomatoes, onions and tuna in countless Latin American youth hostels. (I'm realising rather a lot of these memories involve tinned tuna.)

e) My best friend returning from a year abroad in Naples and teaching me the delights of pasta *without* sloppy sauce (or tuna). We were nineteen. I remember her slowly frying onions and courgettes in good olive oil, then coating properly *al dente* pasta with the contents of the frying pan, loads of salt, black pepper and Parmesan, then watching *Roman Holiday* with this happy bowlful, and thinking there was nowhere I'd rather be.

f) Discovering *minestra*, the thick soup/stew to be found in Italy, in which (usually short) pasta is submerged in a pulsey gloop of lentils, chickpeas, beans or even potatoes. I can't remember the exact moment I first ate *pasta e ceci* (with chickpeas), but I can tell you that there is no dish more soothing and satisfying in its plainness than this.

g) The eye-opening moment when I first made Marcella Hazan's 3-ingredient pasta sauce with tomato, butter and white onion. Perfection.

h) Freddie suggesting a visit to 'this shop where they sell fresh pasta in South End Green' one day in our early acquaintance. We walked into a tiny Romagnan emporium called Giocobazzi's. That was the day I realised that I loved him with all my stomach. He bought a box of gorgonzola and walnut ravioli and, back home, coated it with melted butter, sage leaves and a lot of pecorino. This has become a Saturday ritual. (We've both gone up a clothes size since we met.)

i)   Making lasagne with my friend Tim Siadatan at his north London restaurant, Trullo, and pumpkin ravioli in Rachel Roddy's Roman kitchen. This is when things started to get serious and pasta went from a nourishing plaything to culinary aspiration.

Pasta has punctuated my life in eating. Unfilled and in its dried state – the form with which I grew up – it is essentially a blank canvas onto which the cook can cast their whims and curiosities. For this reason, I think of pasta as the food that taught me how to cook. I have spent many evenings throwing whatever ingredients I have to hand into a pan of 'pasta sauce': the oil from a tin of anchovies, or the dregs of some white wine, or a teaspoon of Marmite, or ageing chillies, or wilting herbs . . . It is the perfect base upon which to practise improvisational cooking, capable of carrying any ingredient and an ideal bed to test whether two or more flavours are natural partners. What's more, unless I've over-salted the sauce, it's fairly easy to claw yourself out of a Pastagate situation.

Some of my greatest pasta triumphs have been mistakes. Either because I hadn't been shopping and pasta is my immediate fall-back, or because I had planned to cook something else entirely and messed it up . . . and pasta is my immediate fall-back. To borrow the words of Laurie Colwin in her essay, 'Alone in the Kitchen with an Eggplant', these dishes probably do reveal 'man [woman] at his [her] weirdest', but I'm okay with that.

Still, as with any good relationship, mine with pasta is always happiest when we keep things simple. Much as you might think a flavourless fragment of flour and water might need extensive embellishment, the simple fact is that pasta needs little more than a fat base, seasoning and one other thing. Here are some of my favourite combinations for pasta sauce:

1. Marcella Hazan's aforementioned sauce of 3 ingredients (tinned tomatoes, white onion, butter)
2. Green herbs, chilli, Parmesan
3. Anchovy, caper, olive, tomato, chilli, wine
4. Romanesco cauliflower, pecorino, lemon
5. Fresh tomatoes, smoky aubergine, basil
6. Pesto (of any description – see recipe on pages 275–276)
7. Tinned tomatoes, red onion, tuna ('for old time's sake')
8. Tinned tomatoes, cinnamon, garlic
9. Jane Baxter's Bolognese (the best – see recipe on pages 71–73)
10. Courgette, onion, ricotta, Parmesan
11. Broccoli and ricotta
12. Peas, yoghurt, lemon

If you'll excuse one final list, here is some essential advice on cooking pasta:

1. Use the biggest pan you have, to give your pasta the highest water-to-starch ratio possible. This will stop the water temperature dropping too much when the pasta is added to the pan (otherwise, if the water takes a while to get back up to boiling point, the pasta will become soggy and sticky).

2. Salt your water amply. We often hear that pasta water should be as salty as the sea. This is partly for seasoning's sake – pasta usually contains no salt itself, so absorbs the salt as it boils – but also because you want 'coherent' pasta noodles which don't stick together. Salt prevents this.

3. Hold back some of your starchy and salty pasta cooking water to loosen up sauces and make them go further – you want as much flavour in a sauce as possible, so this is better than just adding water.

4. Don't leave your pasta draining for too long – you want a little of the briny water still clinging to it when you serve. Also, don't rinse your pasta! You want some residual starch so that your sauce, ragu or topping wraps itself around it.

5. Keep Parmesan and pecorino rinds and cook them into your sauces where appropriate – this will add an extra layer of umami and salt.

6. Recognise the strengths and weaknesses of certain shapes for different uses: short pasta like ditalini for minestra and soups, long pasta like spaghetti or tagliatelle to coat with oily ragu, tubular pasta to scoop up very saucy sauces.

All the pasta recipes that follow use 100g of pasta to serve one person.

TOMATO 'RED' SAUCE

I make pasta pomodoro more than anything else. This might suggest I had the recipe nailed, but I've never made the same one twice. Below is therefore both a guesstimate and a base with which you can tinker – with herbs, spices, vegetables, anchovies, you name it . . . More often than not, I'll do an even simpler version, with either garlic and olive oil for a sauce with a more southern Italian vibe, or onion and butter for something more northern. Try both! I use the southern kind as my workhorse and keep the buttery version for days when I want (modest) luxury.

SERVES 2–4

4 tbsp extra virgin olive oil

2 onions, finely chopped

2 garlic cloves, finely chopped

2 x 400g tins of whole tomatoes

1 tsp sugar (optional)

grated Parmesan or pecorino, to serve

salt and black pepper

------

1. Heat 3 tablespoons of the oil in a heavy-based saucepan, add the onions and fry gently for 10 minutes or so – let them take their time over this. They need to be soft and developing some colour when you add the garlic. Once the garlic is added, fry for a further 2 minutes.

2. Drain the excess liquid from the tinned tomatoes and add them to the pan, removing any tough tomato tops. Add the remaining tablespoon of olive oil, season with salt and pepper, and briefly

bring to the boil. Once bubbling, turn the heat down very low, so it reaches a steady simmer.

3. Cook the sauce for at least an hour, allowing any excess liquid to evaporate, then remove from the heat and blitz with a hand blender. Return to the heat for a further 15 minutes.

4. When you're ready to eat – you'll have cooked your pasta at this point, reserving a cup of the cooking liquid – taste the sauce. You might want to add more salt, and you might also want a little more sweetness, in which case add some sugar. If the sauce seems a little dry, or you're worried there isn't enough, fear not: add a splash of the pasta water. Slap over your pasta and eat with plenty of black pepper and Parmesan or pecorino.

SPAG BOL

There are certain cooks whose recipes I trust intrinsically, and which are really worth following to the letter. Jane Baxter is one of them, and this is her bolognese recipe, published in Guardian Cook *in May 2014. It's definitely one you need to go out shopping for – the two different types of mince, the pancetta, the cooking wine – but it's worth it.*

———

SERVES 6

1 tbsp butter

1 tbsp olive oil

1 onion, finely chopped

2 carrots, finely chopped

2 celery sticks, finely chopped

100g pancetta or smoked streaky bacon, finely chopped

3 garlic cloves, crushed

250g beef mince

250g pork mince

sprig of thyme

100ml red wine

1 x 400g tin of chopped tomatoes

1 tbsp tomato purée

250ml chicken stock

250ml whole milk

400g dried spaghetti or tagliatelle

grated Parmesan, to serve

salt and black pepper

———

1. Melt the butter with the oil in a large, heavy-based saucepan over a medium heat, then add the vegetables and pancetta and cook for about 10 minutes, until soft. Add the garlic and cook for a further minute, then increase the heat and add both types of mince and the thyme.

2. Brown the meat in the pan for a few minutes, breaking it up with a wooden spoon, then add the wine. Stir well and let the wine reduce while you scrape the bottom of the pan with a wooden spoon.

3. Add the remaining ingredients, except the pasta and Parmesan, and season the mix well. Bring to the boil, then simmer for 1 hour – adding a little extra milk if necessary.

4. Cook the pasta in a large saucepan of generously salted boiling
   water according to the packet instructions, until al dente. Drain well
   and toss with the hot sauce and a little grated Parmesan. Serve.

TAGLIATELLE WITH ROMANESCO, PECORINO AND LEMON

*Romanesco looks like the punky love child of cauliflower and broccoli,
its gaudy green florets peaking into turrets, its flesh soft and sweet.
Half of it is made into a sauce here, a flavourful cloak for long pasta,
while the rest – gently fried with some garlic – crowns each plateful.*

SERVES 4

1 small romanesco cauliflower, broken into florets

400g tagliatelle (or pappardelle, fettuccine, linguine or spaghetti)

5 tbsp extra virgin olive oil, plus extra to serve

1 garlic clove, bashed but left whole

grated zest and juice of ½ unwaxed lemon

100g pecorino, grated, plus extra to serve

salt and black pepper

----

1. Bring a large saucepan of generously salted water to the boil, add the romanesco florets and cook for 5 minutes or so. You want them to hold their shape so be wary of over-cooking them. Once cooked, remove the florets from the water with a slotted spoon and set aside.

2. Keep the water boiling and add the pasta.

3. While the pasta is cooking, heat 2 tablespoons of the olive oil in a frying pan, add the garlic clove and fry over a medium heat for 1 minute. Remove the garlic and tumble in half of the romanesco florets with a good pinch of salt. Fry for 10–15 minutes so that the romanesco takes on a little colour but does not lose its shape.

4. Blitz the remaining romanesco florets and any stems in a food processor or blender with the remaining olive oil, the lemon zest and juice, the pecorino and some seasoning. You should have a very thick, pale green sauce. Transfer the sauce to a large bowl and add a spoonful or 2 of the pasta cooking water to loosen it up a bit.

5. Once the pasta is cooked, drain and toss in the sauce. Divide the pasta between bowls then scatter over the fried romanesco florets, drizzle with oil, scatter with more grated pecorino, and grind some black pepper over each bowl. Serve.

PASTA WITH COURGETTES AND RICOTTA

This can also be made without the ricotta, in which case be a bit more liberal with the olive oil, both when you cook the vegetables and on serving. You could also add a bit of butter for good measure.

———

SERVES 2

2 tbsp extra virgin olive oil, plus extra to serve

1 garlic clove, peeled, bashed, but left whole

1 onion, finely chopped

2 courgettes, cut into 1cm discs

200g pasta

125g ricotta cheese

juice of ½ lemon

grated Parmesan, to taste

a few basil leaves

salt and black pepper

———

1. Heat the olive oil in a large frying pan over a medium heat. Add the garlic and let it release its aroma for a couple of minutes, being careful not to let it burn or colour too much. Remove and discard the garlic – you just want a wink of it in the oil – then add the onion.

2. Cook the onion for 1–2 minutes, until it starts to soften, then tip in the chopped courgettes and cook, stirring frequently, for 5–10 minutes.

3. Meanwhile, cook the pasta in a large saucepan of generously salted boiling water according to the packet instructions, until al dente. As it nears the end of cooking, take a spoonful of the cooking water and add it to the onions and courgettes in the pan, so that they soften and a sauce is created.

4. Beat together the ricotta, lemon juice, a generous handful of grated Parmesan, a big pinch of salt and black pepper, and a small ladleful of pasta cooking water.

5. Drain the pasta, keeping a little bit of pasta water back in case you need more liquid, then combine it with the ricotta mix, tossing everything together. Check the seasoning and add half of the courgette and onion, together with most of the basil leaves, tossing again. Top off each bowl with a generous spoonful of the remaining vegetables, a generous sprinkling of Parmesan, a drizzle of oil, and black pepper. Throw the remaining basil leaves on top and serve.

PASTA WITH MARMITE

More store-cupboard than the store-cupboard pasta recipe to follow, I have never known a better late night snack than this one. It is an Anna Del Conte creation, one that came into being 'by chance'. I love all its component parts and, if you think about it, the marriage of pasta, fat, and two agents of umami, Marmite and Parmesan, makes absolute sense. I'm rather more generous with the Marmite — and the butter, for that matter — than Anna so adjust the quantities to your taste. You won't look back.

———

SERVES 2

200g pasta

30g wedge of butter

1 heaped tsp Marmite

grated Parmesan, to serve

black pepper

———

1. Cook the pasta in a large saucepan of generously salted boiling water according to the packet instructions, until al dente. Just before you drain it, reserve a cup-full of the cooking water. As the pasta drains in the colander, set to work on the saucy bit.

2. Melt the butter (in the same pan that you cooked the pasta in) with the Marmite and pour in the reserved pasta cooking water, then tip the drained pasta back into the pan. Toss it around to coat the pasta completely, then transfer to bowls or plates, cover with a healthy mound of Parmesan and a grinding of black pepper, with more of both on the side.

STORE-CUPBOARD PASTA

I suppose this is a riff on puttanesca, but it's really just a last resort supper. It uses a handful of ingredients that I always have on hand to stand in for lacklustre fridge contents. Onions and garlic aren't strictly 'store-cupboard' I suppose, but I am never without either. They live in a basket in my kitchen on a bed of the crispy shed skins from onions and garlics past. So, really, it's only the herbs you might want to buy, but even if you don't, there's more than enough flavour here, the brawny kapow *of salt and umami and cooked-down booze collaborating to satisfy. You could throw in some fresh tomatoes if you wanted and, if you happen to have braised any vegetables in olive oil recently, this oil recycled makes a delicious sweet base.*

———

SERVES 4–6

extra virgin olive oil, for frying

2 onions, finely chopped

500g pasta (preferably long)

4 garlic cloves, finely chopped

pinch of dried chilli flakes

6 anchovy fillets, and some of their oil

handful of capers, rinsed thoroughly and chopped

handful of olives, pitted and chopped (optional)

glass of white wine

100g Parmesan or pecorino, grated, or to taste

large handful of fresh basil or parsley leaves, torn

salt and black pepper

———

1. Heat 3–4 tablespoons of oil (a generous glug) in a large frying pan over a medium heat, then add the onions. Add a pinch of salt (this helps release some of the liquid in the allium, breaking it down and helping it soften more quickly) and cook for a couple of minutes until the onions are soft but not coloured.

2. Cook the pasta in a large saucepan of generously salted boiling water according to the packet instructions, until al dente.

3. While the pasta is cooking, add the garlic and chilli flakes to the onions and cook for a further 2 minutes then add the anchovies, anchovy oil, capers, olives, if using, and wine. Cook over a low–medium heat until the anchovy fillets have broken down and the pan emits a scent of winey, salty, garlicky joy.

4. Add a glug more oil to the frying pan, a large cup of the pasta cooking water, a grinding of black pepper and the grated Parmesan or pecorino. Drain the pasta and add it to the pan with the torn herbs, tossing the whole lot around. Serve straight away, with more grated cheese and black pepper on top.

Nature

——— . ———

Recently I was cajoled into abandoning my yogic plans in
favour of an evening walk. Admittedly it was a beautiful
summer's evening, one that would have been wasted on forcing
my hamstrings into unnatural positions. (And indeed on
forgoing alcohol, I thought, as I remembered that bottle of
something from Sicily which was in the fridge.)

So we piled off to Hampstead Heath, a wonderful and curious
place in London. On an evening like that you can look upon
the city from Parliament Hill – the shapes of the Gherkin, the
Shard and St Paul's like cartoonish pots of condiment – and feel
at once within it and absolutely set apart from it. This feeling
was pronounced yesterday as we walked further into north
London's tangle – grasses long and golden, kissed by evening
rays. There was an intensely grounding smell in the air.

I sniffed, and sniffed, and sniffed again. I felt like I was
somewhere else, but I couldn't put my finger on where that scent

of drying grass and what-I-imagine-to-be-photosynthesis-but-who-knows-if-it-actually-is transported me to as I ran through the gamut of recent holidays and childhood trips abroad. It's the sun, I thought, it must be the sun. The sun is so other to Londoners that it always feels borrowed.

Now, Freddie and I both have strong squints. I noticed how, in that evening sun, his Simian brow had flattened just like his dad's, and then realised – peering up at the hint of tuft just above my line of vision – that mine had done the same. My own dad once pointed out how my sun squint is a lot like his own – I like how the weather bears these inherited traits for all to see – and as we walked past the brambles that were still green and hard and only hinting at what they will one day be, come September, I also realised that I felt nowhere else other than at home.

The smell was the smell of stamping on wheat stumps during the Norfolk harvest. It was squinting in the glare that the burning sun creates as it bounces off wheat that bobs in the breeze. It was tomatoes taken from the greenhouse and eaten with black pepper only, probably in the garden, on plastic furniture. It was picking raspberries from the pick-your-own field up the road, and it was the scent the wind carries through the car window as we race back home to stain our fingers and lips with them. It was spending long summers with my granny, summers which I savoured because even then I suspected that such plain satisfaction could never last. It was going to bed in the evening and knowing tomorrow will bring with it the same simple pleasures.

That's got to be better than a yoga class.

* * *

I found that walk particularly powerful because I was experiencing it with Freddie, and it gave me the excuse to divulge little details about my summers with Granny, things I might never have thought to tell him. It was a meeting of worlds – childhood and adult – bridged by a summer's evening.

But while food does of course have the ability to trigger emotional time travel, I think the way I felt on Hampstead Heath that evening hints at something beyond reminiscence. It drew my attention to how things that occur naturally can – from sun-dried grass and mowed lawn mulch to tomato vines and ripe raspberries – nurture the spirit, transcending the five senses. I felt coddled by the breeze flapping through green horse chestnut leaves, and grounded by the toasted grass with its golden perfume. Mother Nature was at work. This isn't a new idea; just look at "The Corners of the Mouth (Providing Nourishment)" in the *I Ching* (or *Book of Changes*) – the ancient Chinese divination text. It shows a diagram of the mouth drawn in horizontal lines, explaining: 'Nourishment of oneself, specifically of the body, is represented in the three lower lines, while the three upper lines represent nourishment and care of others, in a higher, spiritual sense.'

For millennia, then, food has been associated with nurture. Now, it is only since writing this that I've really appreciated the idea of 'Mother Nature'. I used to think it a saccharine euphemism like 'the birds and the bees', or 'passing away', even the premise of storks delivering babies – an almost neo-Victorian term used to explain to children what adults didn't want to – sex, death, and less savoury facts of life. As I've thought more about that evening on Hampstead Heath, though, and all the times I have felt most at peace in the last year, they all involve nature: grounding and maternal. Nature, then, is a kind of mother and, like all good ones, she knows how to put good food on the table.

Nature provides what we eat, of course, though this is all too easily forgotten. When I was at university, I subsisted on a diet of pasta and chickpeas, sometimes separately, and sometimes together. I'll never forget when a friend came into the kitchen at one halls of residence and asked, curiously, 'What are chickpeas made of?' We all laughed, but in the world of today, was that really such a silly question? It just shows how far we've drifted from knowing where our food comes from. It can be especially easy to forget this when you live in the city. Ingredients arrive prepped for us – plucked chickens, vacuum-packed smoked mackerel, washed bags of salad – and we are easily put off by reminders of their previous lives: bugs on lettuce, mud on carrots, blood on meat. I don't have the space to grow anything at home in London, save for a few herbs for cooking – such as bay, sage, mint – but still, it feels like a low maintenance way of connecting with nature, modestly reminding me of the source of what I eat.

Alice Waters

As far as Alice Waters is concerned, gardening is endemic to human nature. The organic, slow-rearing of food is in our genes. I stole an hour with her at Chez Panisse – her legendary restaurant in Berkeley, California. It was an afternoon in June 2015, the day before they held a fundraiser for The Edible Schoolyard, Waters' charity project aimed at giving children at the city's Martin Luther King Jnr school an 'edible education'. The school has a garden and kitchen to teach kids about where their food comes from, how to use it and, more broadly, to enrich their education and senses with the power of nature. For Waters, who as a young woman trained to be a Montessori teacher, a child's sensory education is the most important aspect to their learning, though it remains absent from the school curriculum: 'We need to educate children's senses. That means preparing the garden with aromatic things, with mints and orange blossom, sage, rosemary . . . The kids who have become part of The Edible Schoolyard know the names of all the plants, and feel that they are their friends. Nature has stopped being scary, the unknown.' Since its inception in 1995, the program has gone national, has travelled to Washington DC and been espoused by Michelle Obama. It's a big deal.

I'd ostensibly met up with Waters to talk about her culinary

inheritance – both her own relationship with food via her parents when she was a child, and also what she has passed down to her daughter, Fanny. But her sense of maternal responsibility goes beyond immediate family. Waters sees a weakness in modern American culture – and across the West: a deficit in children's interaction with the nature. And she's tackling it head-on herself. Deodorants, windows that can't be opened, packaged and fast foods . . . all are sanitising forces that brainwash people to think things should always be fast, cheap, easy and convenient. 'This goes against our nature,' says Waters, 'but it's an addiction.' This is also a concern for Richard Louv in his book *Last Child in the Woods*: 'as the young spend less and less of their lives in natural surroundings, their senses narrow, physiologically and psychologically, and this reduces the richness of human experience.'

It is as though the accoutrements of modern life – social media, gaming, processed foods, chemical products and the like – are drugs, compulsive distractions from our purest, happiest selves. For Waters it is simple: 'Nature is both the goodness within us – which helps us to survive physically and spiritually – and around us. We must nurture this nature.' Jung wrote something similar, referring to his idea of the 'natural mind', 'the sort of mind which springs from natural sources, and not from opinions taken from books; it wells up from the earth like a natural spring, and brings with it the peculiar wisdom of nature.' Waters, Louv and Jung all point towards nature nourishing our intuitive and creative skills. The more time we spend in the natural world, the better conditioned we are to be at our most imaginative best.*

Then Alice said something that made me better understand

---

* And, as BBC arts editor Will Gompertz wrote in *Think Like An Artist*, 'It is by being creative that we are likely to find contentment in our digitised age.'

the idea of 'Mother Nature': when kids are connected with nature, she said, they feel it's their mother. Our union with the natural world provides a sense of belonging, a grounding force. Although she doesn't think it necessarily has to be nature in relation to food (swimming in a lake is just as valid as picking mushrooms in a wood to cook with), Waters did acknowledge that 'by making a connection to nature through eating, you digest the values of it.' Perhaps, then, we better process the benefits of being in the natural world if it directly nourishes our bodies via our stomachs.

When I ask her if she was actively trying to pass something of this down to her own daughter, she said there was no question, yes, of course. She comes back to her Montessori training, saying how she appealed to Fanny's senses. 'I prepared a garden for her . . . herbs, flowers, wild strawberries, a bean house . . . and she very quickly became an omnivore. She now never declines a chance to try food.' Waters opened her daughter's eyes not only to the plants and natural wonders of their garden, but also its tastes.

Of course, she has also now done this for the children of Berkeley and beyond. Waters' inspiration for launching The Edible Schoolyard was manifold. She was one of four children, brought up in post-war New Jersey. Her parents cooked and grew vegetables out of necessity but were not food enthusiasts. Her mother used a lot of frozen veg and canned fruit, but also occasional joints of meat, and produce like corn and tomatoes (eaten with lashings of butter and salt) that they had grown in their own Victory Garden.* She remembers a childhood

---

* An initiative set up by President Roosevelt during the Second World War, to encourage civilian Americans to raise food, both for their own consumption and to send to soldiers. Alice Waters' parents kept theirs after the war, even when they moved from New Jersey to Berkeley to be nearby. Waters is now trying to revitalise the movement in the States.

of remarkable freedom spent climbing trees, riding bikes, exploring the woods. The only unbending house rule was that all four children were to be home in time for dinner. 'The last generation to have that kind of freedom, and to grow up knowing what plants were, was mine, and I feel both lucky and sad about that. I never did anything but play outside and we didn't have a TV. Now I think that getting kids into parks is the single most valuable thing for society.'

Her other great influence, and one that has been well-documented, is Europe. Waters has often cited her move to France aged nineteen as being her most important catalyst for change. She became interested in what we now understand to be 'slow food', which was written into everyday behaviour around food in France; where everyone bought local fresh bread each day and ate seasonal food, grown nearby, in neighbourhood restaurants. It changed everything, from her value system to her appetites. 'Taste came into my life,' she says. Later, in 1968, she did her Montessori training – for three- to six-year-olds – in London, just by Hampstead Heath. Fast food culture hadn't yet hit UK shores and barrow markets were still here. 'I used to go to Harrods and marvel at the game, the wild birds, the beautiful fish and oysters, and I used to go to Elizabeth David's shop in Pimlico for blackcurrant jelly. I cooked at home a lot in England.' What she describes is a world in which wild and native British produce was a given, ubiquitous even. The same produce is available now to my generation, albeit in luxury shops and at prohibitive prices. In fact, I write this on the eve of the glorious twelfth,* when only the first grouse of the season

---

* The name given to the 12th August, which marks the beginning of the shooting season – namely of grouse – in the UK.

will become available in restaurants for those whose pockets are deep enough. (Nowadays, with food, timing is a luxury.)

It was interesting to hear Waters' thoughts on English food culture, which I've grown up to see as so inferior to France, Italy, Spain and, latterly, California. In her eyes, we have here a strong gardening movement – evidenced by the very existence of urban allotments – and a history of writing about it, which she says has influenced her. Likewise Italy, where, she says, gardening is an extension of gastronomy.

An in-depth discussion of Alice Waters' mother's cooking never happened, but a deeply maternal quality is never far from her food. I heard the message loud and clear: Nature is our mother, she nurtures us. We must reciprocate this, to keep her well for future generations, and to feed our own bodies and spirits. And, as the mouthpiece for all this, Waters is ever-deserving of her nickname, the mother of American food.

Pulses

— ✀ —

Aptly named pulses are the beating heart of my diet. I'm sure I grew up taking them for granted. Perhaps in this sense they epitomise not just my mother's cooking but the essence of mothers' cooking itself: steady and unremarkable until you move away and realise (a) how good it is, (b) the skill involved in putting seemingly plain things on the table, and (c) how good, straightforward home-cooked food acts as a sounding board against which everything we go on to eat in life is judged.

As a childhood vegetarian, pulses were never far away. Kidney bean-laced chillies in winter, summers of cold puy lentils, and a fridge perennially loaded with hummus in different forms (some things never change). But it was only when I went up to Leeds for university, armed with one of my mother's famous 'survival packs', that I really learned how indispensible pulses can be. (The word 'survival' is used loosely here. My little cousin Layla's pack contained a garlic bulb, a tampon, a toy hamster and £2.50 to buy the Saturday *Guardian* on her first weekend at university.) In mine, she'd included an array of negligibly essential items, some – true to form – more useful than others. At the time, I assumed she'd just had too many chickpeas in her own cupboard so offloaded a tin into mine. It was only towards the end of term when I was out of cash that

I realised the wisdom of this tin of chickpeas; in this instance, the survival pack lived up to its name. I had an onion and a garlic clove, and I can remember nicking a sprig of rosemary from somebody's front garden in Headingley. Slowly fried up together, these four ingredients became the basis for many of my student meals, sometimes with the addition of chopped tomatoes to be eaten with rice, at others bulked out with vegetable bouillon and pasta for a hearty Italian soup. What I'd previously considered uncharismatic tins of beige became vital to my kitchen armoury.

Of course, there's more to chickpeas than tins, and there are more to pulses than chickpeas. Pulses are the edible seeds of legumes, or plants that produce peas in pods. It's a big family of ingredients and, like all successful big families, it knows how to feed many mouths thriftily – without compromising on flavour or variety. In my cooking, I barely skim the surface of pulse varieties (I never cook with aduki or mung beans, for example) but my favourites include chickpeas, lentils, cannellini, kidney beans, borlotti . . . When I haven't given cooking much thought and need a quick fix of protein to pad out a stew or to make a quick and rudimentary dip, a tin of one pulse or another is a great thing to have. Jars are superior (with good deli brands – I like Spanish ones – you'll get lovely fat *garbanzos* with a buttery texture and a flavour that's more pronounced), but not always preferable – for some recipes (like the dip and pasta with beans recipes that follow), the softened consistency of tinned beans is ideal.

Before I started writing about food, I went through a phase of wanting to write a screenplay and, as part of my research, read Robert McKee's seminal text, *Story*. He argues that characters are established on their conflicts, on an inherent clash between their conscious and unconscious desires. This, says McKee, is what makes for a compelling character, and over the course of a script, that conflict is resolved. Perhaps it's going too far to endow the edible seeds of leguminous plants with conscious and unconscious desires, but as a group of ingredients, pulses are curiously full of contradictions: basic, yet luxurious; ancient, but modern (trendy even); unassuming, yet able to assume so many guises; easy to cook with, but a bit of a slog; light, but strangely stodgy; thirsty, amply watered yet, still, peculiarly dry in the mouth. It's these contradictions that keep them interesting. As you'll see from some of my favourite recipes here, they certainly make for dishes with compelling characters.

WHITE BEAN AND OLIVE OIL DIP

A lazy and incidental spin on hummus. I especially like using butter beans because, as their name might suggest, they become really creamy when blended, but cannellini beans work well too. You could cook the beans from dried (in which case it is nice to boil them with a bay leaf to infuse the water), but when I have people over I'm usually flapping over a main course so use tinned. On these occasions, it is useful to have this up my sleeve, for an easy dunking scenario.

——

SERVES 2–4

1 x 400g tin of butter beans, cannellini beans or other white beans, drained (or about 100g dried beans, soaked overnight and cooked until tender, then drained – reserve some bean cooking water)

grated zest of ½ unwaxed lemon

1 garlic clove

2 tbsp extra virgin olive oil, plus extra for drizzling

3 sprigs of basil, dill or parsley, leaves only

salt and black pepper, to taste

——

1. Place all the ingredients in a processor along with a small splash of warm water (or reserved bean cooking water) and blitz for about 20 seconds, until smooth. Spoon into a bowl to make a mountain of dip and drizzle some extra virgin olive oil over its peak. Serve with crudités, pitta, whatever.

BUTTER BEAN AND TUNA SALAD

This would be best with butter beans soaked from dry because they hold their shape better than tinned (which can become mushy), but then it wouldn't be quite the quick fix it's intended to be. This is a faithful alternative to sandwich-based meals — picnics, fast lunches, bare-cupboard days. I'm not fussy about whether the tuna is in oil or brine, but I always buy tinned tuna steak rather than chunks.

SERVES 2–4

1 x 400g tin of butter beans, drained

1 x 120g tin of tuna steak (in oil or brine), drained

1 red onion, finely chopped

1 tbsp extra virgin olive oil

grated zest and juice of ½ unwaxed lemon

handful of parsley, finely chopped (optional)

salt and black pepper, to taste

----

1. Combine the butter beans and tuna in a bowl, breaking up the tuna as you go.

2. Stir in the onion and simply add the remaining ingredients. Toss the mixture into the dressing and leave to sit at room temperature for 30 minutes or so, to give the flavours a chance to come together.

HOME-MADE BAKED BEANS

'Why would you bother to make your own when Heinz do such a good job?', I hear you ask. Because this ticks all the same comfort boxes, but goes bigger on flavour: spice, sweet, sour. Baked beans on acid, quite literally.

———

SERVES 4

250g dried cannellini beans

2 tbsp extra virgin olive oil

2 onions, finely chopped

2–3 garlic cloves, finely chopped

1 tsp curry powder

½ tsp pimentón or paprika

1 heaped tsp tomato purée

1 x 400g tin of chopped or whole tomatoes

3 tbsp red or white wine vinegar

3 tbsp light brown sugar

salt and black pepper

———

1. Cover the cannellini beans in cold water and leave to soak overnight.

2. The next day, drain the beans and transfer them to a large saucepan. Cover them with water and bring to boil. Lower the heat to a lively simmer, cook for 1 hour, then drain, return to the pan with fresh water and bring to boil again, reducing to a simmer and cooking the beans until tender.

3. Heat the olive oil in a heavy-based saucepan over a medium heat and, once it starts to glisten, tip in the onions with a pinch of salt. Cook for 2 minutes, then add the garlic and cook for a few more minutes, stirring frequently, until soft.

4. Add the curry powder, pimentón or paprika, tomato purée, the tomatoes (swirling water into the tin to extract every last bit of tomato and adding this to the pan), vinegar, sugar and some salt and pepper. If using whole tinned tomatoes, break them up in the pan with the side of a spoon.

5. Cook over a medium–high heat for 5 minutes, then add the drained beans and warm them through in the sauce. You could eat this straight away but ideally it's best left to sit for a few hours so the flavours have a chance to come together. Serve on buttered rye toast. Few comforts surpass this.

PASTA E FAGIOLI E CECI

A store-cupboard version of two Italian classics – pasta and beans, and pasta and chickpeas – brought together in my kitchen when I had four mouths to feed and a tin each of borlotti beans and chickpeas.

SERVES 4–6

6 tbsp extra virgin olive oil, plus extra for drizzling

1 onion, finely chopped

1 celery stick, finely chopped

1 carrot, finely chopped

1 bay leaf

sprig of rosemary

1 garlic clove, finely chopped

1 x 400g tin of borlotti beans, drained

1 x 400g tin of chickpeas, drained

1 tbsp tomato purée

1.5 litres water

Parmesan rind or 50g Parmesan, grated

200g small pasta shapes (such as dittalini)

salt and black pepper

———

1. Heat the olive oil in a large frying pan over a low heat. Add the onion, celery, carrot, bay leaf and rosemary. Cook gently for about 10 minutes, then add the garlic and cook for a further 2 minutes. You should have a soft, fragrant soffritto mix.

2. Add the drained beans, chickpeas and tomato purée and give the whole mixture a good stir, coating everything in everything. Add the water and Parmesan rind (if you don't have this, then add the 50g of Parmesan later in step 4), bring to the boil, then reduce the heat and simmer for 15 minutes.

3. Remove and discard the bay leaf, rosemary and Parmesan rind, if using. Roughly blitz the bean mixture with a hand blender: you want it to be half-blended – a thick gloop with plenty of whole beans within it.

4. Add the pasta to the pan and cook until al dente. Keep a watch over the pan – you may need to add a splash of water. If you didn't add Parmesan rind, now add the 50g of Parmesan, season to taste and serve with extra virgin olive oil on the table for people to swirl on top.

SPICED FISH
AND BEANS

Honey and Co's hake in 'fake' matbuha sauce – published in the very first Cook *residency column – inspired this recipe, although it is not the same as theirs. It is fake, we are told, because* matbuha *('cooked salad' in Arabic) is normally made with fresh peppers, tomatoes and soaked beans in North Africa. And this, as you'll see, is a store-cupboard surprise. I usually make it with chickpeas as they tend to be what I have, but cannellini, borlotti or butter beans would all work well.*

———

SERVES 2

3 tbsp extra virgin olive oil

6 garlic cloves, crushed

1 tbsp ground cumin

1 tsp pimentón

1 tsp ground coriander

1 tsp ground caraway

1 cinnamon stick

pinch of dried chilli flakes

1 tbsp harissa

1 tbsp tomato purée

250ml water

1 unwaxed lemon, quartered
and 1 quarter thinly sliced (skin and all)

1 x 400g tin of beans (your choice), drained and rinsed

pinch of sugar (optional)

300–400g fresh white fish fillet (hake, cod or whiting), cut in half

soft, crusty bread, to serve

salt and black pepper

———

1. Heat the oil in a frying pan over a low heat, then add the garlic and spices and fry, stirring occasionally, for about 2 minutes or until the garlic is cooked and a heady, spicy scent is filling your kitchen. Add the tomato purée, water, the sliced lemon and the beans, stir and bring to a gentle boil.

2. Taste for seasoning – it should be spicy and sour, and just sweet enough. Add salt and, if you need to, a pinch of sugar.

3. Season the fish pieces with salt, then carefully lay them in the bubbling sauce, skin-side up. Cover the pan and leave it over a low heat for 5–6 minutes, until the fish is just cooked through. You can check by inserting a knife or prodding it with the back of a spoon – the fish should have a little bounce, but also flake when you apply more pressure.

4. Crack over some black pepper and serve with soft, crusty bread and lemon quarters.

Where possible, it pays to plan when you cook pulses and to soak them from dried. Try to do this for as long as possible – ideally overnight for chickpeas, and more like four hours for smaller ones – to give them a more even consistency once they're cooked (lentils can manage on just one hour's soaking). Once soaked, give them a rinse, place them in a pan and cover with cold water – the surface of the water should be about a thumb above the pulse (you can add more water later if you need to). I really love to put a bay leaf in the water at this point to infuse the beans with something gently aromatic – bay is one of the essential scents of home cooking for me. Bring to a vibrant boil, then reduce the heat to a gentle simmer until cooked through.

The toughness of a dried pulse is deceptive – don't be fooled. Remember they are delicate little things really: to avoid their skins breaking and to keep them intact, stir them as little as possible while cooking. Only add salt once cooked otherwise you risk the pulse firming up prematurely. When it comes to buying pulses dry, it might be tempting to do so in bulk, but they do become tougher over time and only last for up to a year. So you're better off buying them in more modest proportions, storing them in airtight containers, then replenishing your stash every couple of months.

The following recipes work best with pulses that have been soaked and then cooked.

BRAISED LENTILS

We ate these as the clock struck midnight on New Year's Eve/Day when we were in Sicily. The more you eat, the better your luck for the coming year. I ate loads. Fingers crossed.

———

**SERVES 6 AS A MAIN
OR 10 AS A SIDE**

6 tbsp extra virgin olive oil, plus extra for drizzling

1 onion, finely chopped

1 carrot, finely chopped

1 celery stick, finely chopped

4 garlic cloves, finely chopped

2 bay leaves

500g brown lentils

glass of white wine (optional)

salt and black pepper

———

1. Heat the oil in a heavy-based pan over a low–medium heat, add the onion, carrot and celery and fry gently for 10 minutes, then add the garlic. Continue to fry for a further 3 minutes or so until the mixture is soft and fragrant but has not taken on any colour.

2. Add the bay leaves and the lentils and continue to cook for a minute or 2, stirring to make sure the lentils are coated in the mixture. The bay leaves should start to release their scent too.

3. Cover generously with water, and the wine, if using. The amount of liquid you need will vary according to your lentils. Start with the liquid level reaching 2cm above the lentils (you may well need to add more as you go). Increase the heat, bring to the boil, then reduce to a medium heat and cook at a rumbling simmer.

4. My lentils usually take a bit longer than 30 minutes to cook, though this varies, so keep checking and be ready to add more water.

5. Remove from the heat, season generously with salt and pepper and serve drizzled with olive oil. Also delicious with a blob of natural yoghurt.

3 COCONUT DAHL

I've been told that this recipe sounds like an address. It is certainly the route to a happy stomach. It owes its name to the three forms of coconut it contains — solid oil, desiccated flakes and the milk — which together make it textured, creamy, a little more exotic, and (accidentally) vegan. I grew up with dahl in various forms — usually much more basic assemblages of lentils, onion and curry powder. I'm very fond of curry powder's mild tang, so I've kept that in here. Use red or black lentils and remember they are thirsty (especially the black ones), so monitor your simmering potful, keep stirring and always be at the ready to add more water. Lentils also love salt; many times I've added what seems like too much salt to a potful like this, but they soon absorb it and just taste well-seasoned. The amount of water and salt you use is, of course, up to you. Only you know your salt threshold and ideal texture — I like decipherable lentil rounds within a satisfying gloop. Remember that 'to bring your dahl back to life' as my granny did, simply add more water to it the following day and reheat. It'll be as good as new.

———

SERVES 4

1 onion

3–4 garlic cloves

4cm piece of fresh root ginger, peeled

1 tsp cumin seeds

1 tsp black onion seeds

1 tsp fenugreek seeds

½ tsp dried chilli flakes

1½ tbsp solid coconut oil

3 tbsp desiccated coconut

1 tsp curry powder

1 tsp ground turmeric

250g lentils

1 x 400g tin of coconut milk

800ml–1 litre water, as required

juice of ½ lemon

salt

———

1. Blitz the onion, garlic and ginger together in a blender or chop and grind to a paste using a pestle and mortar.

2. Heat a large, deep sauté pan or heavy-based saucepan over a medium heat, add the cumin seeds, onion seeds and fenugreek seeds and dry fry for a couple of minutes until they become fragrant. Keep stirring them to avoid them burning.

3. Add the chilli flakes and 1 tablespoon of the coconut oil. Once it has melted, add the onion, garlic and ginger mixture. Lower the heat a little and let the mixture sweat for about 7 minutes, until it starts to develop some colour, then add the desiccated coconut and fry gently for a further couple of minutes. Add the curry powder, turmeric, the remaining ½ tablespoon of coconut oil and the lentils. You want them to acquire a glossy coating from the oil. Stir-fry for a minute or 2.

4. Add the coconut milk and 400ml of the water, increase the heat and, once boiling, reduce to a lively simmer. Now it's just a question of careful monitoring. Add water in 100–200ml increments as the liquid is absorbed and keep doing so until your dahl has the consistency you desire. I find it can be up to 1 litre, but you might need more, or much less. Play it by ear.

5. Add plenty of salt to taste and a drizzle of lemon juice and serve with basmati rice and yoghurt.

LENTIL AND TURMERIC RICE FRY

This is a brilliant accompaniment to meat, fish and stews. It's also good eaten cold the next day with salad.

———

SERVES 6–8

250g lentils (I like green)

300g basmati rice

2 tbsp extra virgin olive oil

1 onion, finely chopped

1 tsp ground turmeric

2 garlic cloves, grated

600ml vegetable stock

1 bunch of coriander, finely chopped

salt and black pepper

———

1. Put the lentils in a saucepan, cover with cold water and bring to the boil. Once boiling, reduce the heat to a lively simmer and cook for 15–20 minutes.

2. In the meantime, soak the rice in a bowl of cold water until you need it.

3. Heat 1 tablespoon of the oil in a frying pan over a medium heat, add the onion and cook for 2 minutes, then add the turmeric. Cook over a very low heat until the onion softens and glows yellow from the spice.

4. Check the lentils. They want to be approaching done – i.e. still having a little bite – when you remove them from the heat and drain.

5. Drain the rice and add it to the frying pan along with the garlic, lentils, and the remaining tablespoon of oil, stir to coat and fry so that everything glistens with oil and turmeric. Increase the heat to high, add the stock, and allow it to bubble away for 5 minutes, then stir, turn down the heat to low and cover with a lid or plate. Allow it to cook gently for 10 minutes or so until the rice is cooked and fluffy.

6. Remove the lid, season to taste and fork the coriander through. You're good to go.

LENTIL SHEPHERD'S PIE WITH SWEET POTATO MASH

I kept trying to think of an alternative name for this, one that didn't suggest lamb like 'shepherd's' does. 'Lentil grower's pie' doesn't have quite the same ring to it though.

———

SERVES 6

4 tbsp extra virgin olive oil

2 carrots, finely diced

2 celery sticks, finely diced

1 white onion, finely diced

1 garlic clove, minced

2 bay leaves

500g lentils (I like green)

2.2 litres cold water, or more if required

grated zest of 1 unwaxed lemon, and juice of ½

1 tsp ground white pepper

½ tsp ground cinnamon

½ tsp pimentón

salt, to taste (you will need quite a lot)

For the mash topping

2 sweet potatoes

6 regular potatoes

1 tbsp Dijon mustard

1 tbsp olive oil, plus extra for drizzling

70g grated Cheddar cheese (I use smoked when I have it)

grated Parmesan, to taste

——

1. First make the soffritto. Heat 3 tablespoons of the olive oil in a heavy-based saucepan over a low heat, add the carrots, celery and onion and cook gently for 10 minutes, until softened. Add the garlic and bay leaves and cook for a further 5 minutes.

2. Preheat the oven to 200°C/400°F/Gas mark 6. Add the lentils to the pan with the soffritto and cook for a minute or so, stirring to coat them in the glistening oil.

3. Cover with the water, increase the heat, and bring to boil then reduce the heat and cook at a steady, lively simmer, stirring

occasionally, until tender. Keep an eye on the water level, and add more water if the lentils have absorbed it all and are still tough.

4. Meanwhile, put the sweet potatoes in the oven to roast for about 45 minutes and boil the regular potatoes for 25 minutes, or until tender. You don't need to worry about peeling them. Remove the sweet potatoes from the oven once cooked through, leave to cool for a few minutes, then split and scoop out the orange flesh into a bowl. Drain the regular potatoes thoroughly then add them to the sweet potato.

5. When the lentils are tender but not soft, and have absorbed almost all the water, leaving just a little murky juice lingering around the bottom of the pan, add the lemon zest and juice, pepper, cinnamon, pimentón and remaining olive oil to the lentils, season generously with salt then decant the mixture into an ovenproof pie dish.

6. Mash the potato and sweet potato together and add the mustard, olive oil, cheese and some salt. Spread this evenly across the top of the lentils then top with grated Parmesan. Transfer to the oven and bake for 20 minutes, until bubbling at the sides and brown on top. Eat with chutney and greens.

CHICKPEA, OLIVE AND RAISIN TAGINE

If I were faithful to Moroccan naming traditions, this wouldn't be called a tagine but a cast iron casserole pot, after the vessel in which it is cooked. But that would be long-winded and the opposite of this incredibly straightforward dish. Chickpeas — which I think of as almost meaty — are its backbone, and the caramelised onions, carrots, honey and dried fruits give it a sweetness that's offset by the acidic preserved lemons, umami olives and aromatic spices. There's real complexity of flavour, making it a conveniently low effort showstopper!

———

SERVES 6

800g dried chickpeas

5–6 strands of saffron

50g unsalted butter

4 onions, 1 grated, 3 sliced into half moons

3 tsp ground cinnamon

2 tsp ground ginger

½ tsp freshly grated nutmeg

1 tsp salt

1 tsp ground black pepper

4 carrots, peeled and cut into 2cm chunks

200g raisins or sultanas (I like golden ones best)

about 350g green pitted olives

1 tbsp honey

1 tbsp extra virgin olive oil

1 preserved lemon, pulp removed and rind very thinly sliced

big handful of whole almonds, toasted

1 tsp Ras el hanout (optional)

———

1. Soak the chickpeas overnight in cold water.

2. Make the saffron water by dropping the strands of saffron into a mug and covering with 2 tablespoons of warm water. Leave to infuse for 10 minutes.

3. Melt half the butter in a deep-sided pan or heavy-based ovenproof dish over a low heat. Add the saffron water, grated onion, cinnamon, ginger, nutmeg and salt and pepper. Cook for 10–15 minutes, stirring, until the mixture forms a fragrant paste-like consistency and the onion begins to turn translucent and meld into the spices.

4. Drain the chickpeas, add them to the pan and cover with water to 0.5cm above the chickpeas, cover, increase the heat, bring to the boil, then simmer for 30 minutes, before adding the sliced onions. Simmer for a further 20 minutes.

5. Preheat the oven to 120°C/250°F/Gas mark ½. Check the seasoning of the broth, then add the carrots, raisins and olives and simmer until the carrots are tender (i.e. they hold their shape but are not crunchy).

6. Remove the vegetables, chickpeas and raisins from the broth and place in a heatproof dish. Cover the dish with foil and place in the warm oven.

7. Add the honey, olive oil and remaining butter to the broth, bring to the boil and simmer until it reduces and thickens.

8. Arrange the warm vegetables and chickpeas on a serving dish. spoon the reduced broth over, then sprinkle with preserved lemon pieces, almonds and a little Ras el hanout – if you like – for extra spice and prettiness. Serve with couscous, rice and, if you fancy an injection of dairy goodness, some goat's cheese or feta crumbled on top.

CANNELLINI AND CARROT SALAD

No one dislikes this. The joy of this salad lies in the dressing, which plays on the power of lemon juice to break down the feathered onions into softened, subtly crunchy purple strands sweetened by a little sugar. This coats the cannellini and whatever vegetable you choose to combine with it: I like sautéed carrots, but in summer some chunks of fennel would also be good. In winter you could try some briefly roasted chunks of sweet potato.

As ever, you want really good, peppery extra virgin olive oil.

SERVES 4

250g dried cannellini beans

1 red onion, sliced into half moons

grated zest and juice of 1 unwaxed lemon

1 tbsp sugar

6 tbsp extra virgin olive oil, plus extra for frying

6 carrots, washed, topped and tailed (peeled if you like)

1 bunch of dill, finely chopped

salt

———

1. Put the cannellini beans in a bowl, cover with water and leave to soak for 4 hours.

2. Drain the soaked beans, place them in a saucepan and cover with cold water. You want twice the amount of water to beans. Bring to the boil, then reduce the heat and simmer for 1½–2 hours, until tender.

3. Meanwhile, put the sliced red onion in a medium bowl and cover with the lemon zest and juice, the sugar, olive oil and a pinch of salt. Leave to stand for 1 hour – the red colour of the onion will start to seep into the liquid and they will soften.

4. Cut the carrots diagonally across into chunky pieces no more than 1.5cm thick, and drain the beans.

5. Heat a generous glug of oil in a sauté pan over a medium heat, then add the carrots. Fry for 10 minutes, until they start to soften and develop some colour, then add half the dill. Try a piece of carrot – you want it to still be a little crunchy. Add the drained beans and continue to sauté for a further 2 minutes.

6. Toss in half the onion mixture and the other half of the dill, then arrange on a plate, top with the rest of the onions and drizzle with the remaining onion soaking liquid.

Balance

— · —

To me, recipes are conversations, not lectures.
                                    Ruth Reichl, *My Kitchen Year*

I firmly believe that there is food for the right occasion and time. The need for clarity, and for a single-mindedness about what is right and wrong . . . all this applies to the plate.
                    Yotam Ottolenghi, interviewed in London, November 2015

Every Saturday morning I go to a spinning class up the road. That means riding an exercise bike to thumping music and feeling a kind of damp, burning thigh pain for forty-five minutes. I appreciate I'm not selling it to you, but I like it more than I let on. The Irish instructor plays a lot of Riverdance, a soundtrack that holds great sway in getting me to move (it's amazing what an accelerating folk tempo can inspire). In between sprints and climbs, we are told to return to our 'base resistance', a comfortable gear that doesn't require strenuous exertion but where the leg muscles are still engaged. This point is particular to every individual body – there's no saying that mine will be the same as yours – so we are encouraged to find our own base at the beginning of class. I now know that mine is gear ten. Your 'base' in spinning is a personal comfort zone, normal – or as close to normal as you can get

on a stationary bike in a dark little room with disco lights and Riverdance music.

I think people have a not dissimilar base mode with eating. We all have our comfort foods, the things that keep us satisfied, nourished, ticking over. Like my gear ten, these foods are unchallenging but invigorating; not huge indulgences but more often than not, they are the things I want to eat. They are my happy humdrum – not the dizzy heights of recipe testing or eating out – no, I'm talking spaghetti and tomato sauce, avocado on toast, braised lentils swirled with yoghurt and olive oil, baked potato with Branston pickle, a plate of greens with garlic and a piece of toast, boiled eggs with Marmite soldiers, green salad with vinaigrette. Basically, they're the things I've eaten all my life, and the very definition of comfort food – which should quietly fuel and reassure us. (To my mind, 'comfort food' is not decadent.)

Regularly cooking for the same people is a reminder of this victual base mode. I currently share a home with two people, one (Freddie) whose base is breaded chicken escalope with roast potatoes, and the other who eats, almost nightly, steamed vegetables with supermarket cheese sauce. I find these daily cravings unfathomable. Judgements aside, we all have our own approach to dietary balance, and I know that mine finds its roots on my mother's table. (Freddie's does too, I think. His mum makes superlative roast potatoes, on which he subsisted alongside chicken nuggets for a lot of his childhood – I suppose breaded escalope is a natural progression.) In an ideal world, our parents offer comfort; if our parental experience has been a positive one, then it makes absolute sense that the foods they fed us, the food we learned to eat, is the food to which we naturally return when we seek a steady baseline.

It is perhaps only when we feel unbalanced that we realise how important balance is to feeling good. Finding a route to physical and mental equilibrium is again a personal thing. My Riverdance spin sessions started in an effort to offset my weekday excesses, for example. And just as I will read a novel if I've only been reading about food for a while, I will make something like a vegetable curry if I've only eaten sandwiches at my desk all week. Balance avoids stagnation and overload. It maintains our appreciation for the things we know we like and makes our experience of them the best it can be. This applies to everything, certainly to food, and to cooking as well as to eating.

I think about this idea of balance in two ways with food. Firstly, balancing flavours, a responsibility that lies primarily with the cook, but which the eater can tweak once the food is on their plate. Seasoning is essential here. In *Guardian Cook*, salt is practically the only thing we consistently *don't* provide a specific measurement for in recipes – we leave it up to the reader/cook to make that decision. They must of course consider their personal preference – why serve something that doesn't taste good to you? – but also remember that those eating said dish will have different palates. For this reason, and because over-salting is so hard to undo, I suggest erring on the side of caution and slightly under-salting a dish (the exception here is of course pasta water, see page 69). I also recommend doing this because so many people have the maddeningly stupid habit of adding salt to their plate before tasting what's on it.

Secondly, balance is a question of health. This transcends ideas about 'being healthy'. Understanding ingredients and how to make meals with them is about more than treating your

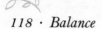

body well. Cooking makes the connection between eating as a physical act and eating as a mental act, addressing the schism between mind and body consciousness that my interview with Susie Orbach raises on page 219. I don't mean over-thinking what you eat (as so many of us in the West are inclined to); I mean seeing food as something you need both physically and imaginatively, and understanding how cooking food for yourself can feed both body and mind.

Yotam Ottolenghi

Look at the ingredients list in any of Yotam Ottolenghi's recipes and they seem to hang in delicate balance. Three-quarters of a tablespoon of red wine vinegar; fifteen basil leaves, shredded; 280g cooked floury potatoes; 65g walnuts, 470g peeled baby shallots.* Once you've completed the daunting task of sourcing some of the lesser-known ingredients, you consider the quantities: the writer's precision implies necessity, as though the fifteenth basil leaf that you just don't have, or a missing 5g of walnuts, will throw the dish in question off kilter. Each recipe is a symphony of ingredients, and each of those ingredients – it seems – needs to be pitch perfect, and at the exact volume directed by the conductor. There is a lot to orchestrate.

Given the nature of his recipes, then, it is at first surprising that Yotam describes himself as a purist. This is a word that, to me, suggests an inherent simplicity. But the food for which Ottolenghi has become famous is neither basic nor straightforward, drawing instead on seemingly boundless and mixed influences, a magician's alchemy. 'Perfectionist', yes, but I'm not sure 'pure' instantly springs to mind.

---

* All measurements lifted from different recipes in *Plenty* and *Plenty More*.

But that's just his cooking. As an eater, Yotam *is* a purist. He is insistent on this: he likes linearity, he likes clarity, and he doesn't like mixing on his plate. He hates Sunday roasts for this reason, for the inevitable, homogenous sea of brown stodge that emerges before him as his plate is piled with a cacophony of different things. Christmas lunch is his idea of horror.

This starts to make sense to me. Only someone with razor-clean, single-mindedness could come up with some of Ottolenghi's concoctions, and this makes order essential. He likes to eat sequentially, like the Italians: salad, then pasta, then meat. His Italian father shares his predilection for order, as does his young son, Max, who separates everything on his plate. Early on, when Max started eating solid food, Yotam observed his son's preference for meat and starch over greens, so Yotam started to emulate the Italian sequence, starting with the greens so he ate them first when he was really hungry. Now they eat together at six o'clock and Yotam revels in the simplicity of their home-cooked meals – 'naked cucumber', avocado, beans, miso, pasta with olive oil and garlic – keeping him in balance with the mayhem of recipe testing, 'of eating more food than I should'.

Balance is important to Ottolenghi and, like most things he puts his mind to, he's good at it. He juggles his London restaurant, deli group, column for the *Guardian,* and string of book projects with his adored family – husband Karl Allen, and their two small sons. On the morning we meet, he's already on his third coffee as I raise my first to my lips at his Soho restaurant, Nopi. Yotam has just participated in a 'salon' at a small 'intentionally untrendy' café in Marylebone. Once a week he gathers there with a group of friends and discusses a current news story. This strikes me as rather like his approach to cooking, but in reverse. Perhaps he needs that same grasp of a situation's ingredients to understand fully the issues it serves up. 'It's an instinct we all have, to ask about what we're doing, whatever that is, and to understand it.'

I ask him about his earliest memories of food. 'It's difficult', he says, 'memories are all so constructed.' He mentions Max again – watching his child develop seems to dredge up echoes of Ottolenghi's childhood self. He describes how he has a Fortnum & Mason chocolate catalogue at home, which Max has named 'The Chocolate Book'. He has assigned attributes to each picture of chocolate within its pages ('this one is spicy' and so on). Max hasn't tried any of these chocolates but, inspired by how they look, he projects flavour characteristics onto them. 'I was the same, I think', says Yotam. Food – namely chocolate – was highly sensual, full of suspense, imaginatively imbued. 'My mum had a Formica-lidded box full of chocolate high up in the kitchen cupboard. I would climb secretly over the counter to get to it, and I remember everything about how it felt: the ritual of tearing the paper, how the chocolate snapped....'

Among his childhood meals, Yotam remembers stews made by the Moroccan woman who looked after him and his siblings, something between a ratatouille and a tagine. Both parents worked, and both cooked. It was over breakfast that the Ottolenghi household ate together most often, and they made it a big thing: toasted bread, raw vegetables, quark cheese, sliced mortadella, his mother's mayonnaise with coriander and garlic . . . Her breakfast spread remains the same to this day. Yotam beams, 'it's just the best.'

His father had the more flexible hours of the two, and would often prepare dinner. He'd heat up milk for the children beforehand, then make nice, simple things: giant couscous (maftoul), fried onions and tomatoes, semolina porridge, pasta. True to his roots, there was always an Italian sensibility to his cooking; he still does things like potatoes fried with rosemary and olive oil, and his interpretation of the chopped Israeli salad is particular, the tomatoes in chunkier, rustic wedges.

Yotam's mother, whose background is German, was always more adventurous in her cooking, less chained to tradition than his father. She'd make Germanic things like cabbage and slow-cooked sausage and, in tune with the times, had Myra Waldo's fashionable American cookbook, *The International Encyclopedia of Cooking*, on her shelves, from which he remembers having Malaysian dishes and Indian curries. 'I'd say my parents actively *didn't* make "Jewish food". In Italy and Germany, the Jewish communities were smaller and more assimilated than in the eastern Mediterranean and North Africa.'

He grew up in Jerusalem at a time when people were encouraged to forget their cultural identities in favour of a new Israeli one. More recently, people have set out to discover their grandmother's food. This isn't always the romantic pursuit it's made out to be, he says, because some dishes just don't need to be made any more (laughing, he quotes a joke he heard, 'You only eat gefilte fish[*] if your grandmother is still alive'), but 'the smart thing that both home cooks and restaurants do is to assimilate those traditions with what's available now. We have such a rich cultural palette from which to pick.' He cites the harissa style sauces from Tripoli as an example: people love them, and they're now mixed into Palestinian food (and, by default, Israeli food too).

---

[*] Gefilte fish is an Ashkenazi Jewish dish of poached white fish like pike or carp, ground up with spices, onion, carrots, sometimes eggs. It is most commonly eaten as an appetiser on Jewish holidays.

We start talking about Israel. One of the problems, he says, was always that official Israeli culture was traditionally based on eastern Europeans, on the Ashkenazi founding fathers, while the Sephardis were considered inferior. 'With food, this was the opposite of the truth, of course, and Sephardi food is what everyone now wants to eat . . . Jewish culture has more or less amalgamated in Israel now, and food culture has really helped with that.' These days, tensions are fewer within the Jewish community but continue, bleakly, between Israelis and Palestinians. Though the two groups are much at odds, their shared food culture is perhaps something of a leveler; as Yotam says 'Food is a safe haven. It's a place where people can act normally when everything else is not very normal at all.'

Yotam's maternal grandparents moved briefly to Sweden in the thirties before emigrating to what was then Palestine in 1939. His grandmother went on to work for the Mossad (the Israeli secret service), but when family was around she cooked insulating German food, like ox tongue simmered in aromatics, and roast potatoes and cauliflower with a bread and butter sauce. 'My grandmother wasn't universally liked, but she *was* universally respected. With role models like her, it made sense to me that you could be both a cook and a working person.' Such dichotomies as male/female, mother/father, breadwinner/cook didn't exist in his family – perhaps another clue to his understanding of balance.

Ottolenghi's paternal, Italian grandparents lived in the suburbs of Tel Aviv. He saw them less often but this seems to have enhanced his memories of eating with them. Best of all he remembers the Roman style semolina gnocchi that his grandmother made, the kind served in layered discs with melted butter and grated cheese. Yotam has been trying to recreate the dish in his London test kitchen recently. Looking at it, he was convinced he'd done a pretty good job, but it tasted incredibly bland, and no one who tried it was particularly enthused.

'I guess it's an illusory memory', he says, 'certain things will never taste as good as they once did. Equally, I can't laugh with the same childish joy at things as Max does.' The thrill of taste experienced for the first time dulls with repetition, then, and as Ottolenghi reflects on this I sense it is exactly that thrill he likes to chase. Is it only through novelty – through new com- binations of carefully measured flavours – that childish delight in eating can be had in adulthood? 'There's something about tasting something for the first time. It's just glorious. After a while you lose the purity of that, the palate naïveté . . .' So, with fifteen basil leaves here and 65g of walnuts there, he just keeps on inventing.

Seasoning

—— ✿ ——

A seasoning is an amplifier that makes things taste more like themselves. Salt and pepper turn up the volume on an ingredient's essence, unlocking and marrying flavours so that they taste as good as possible. To me, the word seasoning – a bit curious at first – makes the most sense in the context of what it can do to an ingredient that's out of season. Think of how a crumbling of Maldon salt flakes and a squeeze of lemon give vibrancy to sullen salad in winter; they bring the out of season into season, from budding to blooming.

Cooks from cold climates with a penchant for tomatoes, for instance, will know the value of seasoning – and likely rely on it. That said, it is often the countries that produce the tomatoes least in need of lifting – Italy, Spain, across the Mediterranean – that seem to know how to use casual flourishes of seasoning to lift them best. How else do you explain the simple happiness of ripe tomatoes, good olive oil, salt and black pepper; tomatoes with meaty anchovies strewn across their cut sides; a Greek salad?

So, what is seasoning? Usually we think just of salt and pepper and, unless otherwise stated, 'season to taste' in recipes refers to this duo. Salt can be your best friend and your worst enemy, a dish's glory when in balance, and its downfall when

that balance is tipped. I can't think of any other agent of flavour through which a measurement so tiny as 'a pinch' can make such a massive difference. (And I mean black pepper; its white counterpart is one that takes more of a headline status. Black pepper does its thing more quietly.)

But there are other ingredients that I often use as seasonings – either to create the deep, founding flavours of a dish or to finish it with a final livening hit. These are often, but not always, salty, mainly because of how they have been preserved (bacon, anchovy, Parmesan), and lend a savouriness that can be preferable to salt for two reasons:

1. Salt has itself already seasoned them, which means there's something else going on. This is usually an animal dimension. Bacon/pancetta are salty, yes, but also taste piggy, smoky and have a fat content – which, if you are frying an onion, for example, founds the flavours both with the salt and the fat it releases. Parmesan has generous quantities of salt added as it is made, but also has the delightful sting of aged milk. And anchovies taste intensely of the sea before being packed in salt or oil.

2. It's harder to over-salt a dish which is seasoned with the likes of bacon, anchovy or Parmesan. We've all been there, shaking table salt from some unwieldy plastic vessel into the pan in question when, suddenly, a white flurry shoots out before you can say 'when'. Said panful is ruined. Over-salting is probably the hardest thing to remedy in cooking, and for this reason I recommend always adding salt by hand. Flaky sea salt like Maldon is great for this, the tactility of crunching it in between fingers giving you a firmer grasp of how much you're putting in. A base of bacon or anchovy,

or a final sleet of Parmesan gives a balanced, moderate and more mature seasoning.

Here, then, are the ingredients I most use to season my food. All are obviously ingredients in their own right:

Anchovy

The divisive anchovy is the reason I cannot countenance becoming vegetarian again.

Eating an anchovy, or anything in which it features, is satisfying whenever you feel a mild carnivorous impulse. It can remind you that you're alive, awakening your palate after a day of dreary eating. In my house, it is a stalwart supper ingredient, particularly useful when we don't have much food in stock.

In her book *An Everlasting Meal*, American food writer Tamar Adler writes about anchovies in her chapter, 'How To Feel Powerful'. There is muscularity to anchovies that makes the cook feel bold. I certainly feel armed when I have a jar of them to hand and am never without one in the fridge. Tins suffice, and are a good budget option, but jars keep better and are better value for money. (You never need a lot of anchovy and it is rare to use a whole jar or tin in one go.)

I also prefer anchovies in oil to anchovies packed in salt. The oil is an ingredient in its own right (it is onion-frying nectar, or great in salad dressings). And I find rinsing the excess salt from anchovies packed in salt to be a bit of a faff.

Too many people don't like anchovies, even some of the eaters I most respect. I tend to use them in the safety of my own home, with a small and close-knit network of vocal enthusiasts. For

this reason, my favourite uses of anchovies are straightforward and quickly thrown together.

1. With eggs. This is winning in so many capacities: laid across toast underneath scrambled or poached eggs; mashed into butter to spread across a boiled egg's soldiers; in devilled/stuffed/Pegasus eggs (see pages 32–33); together in a luxurious take on salsa verde, the list goes on . . .

2. Mixed into butter or mayonnaise (see above).

3. Puttanesca, or an inauthentic equivalent (see store-cupboard pasta on pages 78–79).

4. In a salad with tomatoes and parsley. As simple as it sounds; the triptych of the fish, the fruit, the herb, crowned in good olive oil and black pepper.

5. To dress bitter greens. I love *puntarelle*, the sharp Roman green with a fleeting winter season. This is traditionally eaten with an anchovy and lemon dressing, which would also work well with chicories and radicchio.

6. Bagna cauda, anchoiade and other dips for crudités.

Parmesan and friends

I can remember a dingy time last century when 'Parmesan' meant tubs of ready-grated fluff with a vomitous nose. Luckily those days are behind us and a big wedge of the cheese is both a lovely thing to hack away at neat, and a seasoning that lends a tangy, milky complexity to so many pot and platefuls.

A good, versatile and salty cheese is something I always have around. This usually comes in the form of Parmesan, but I also love slightly funkier pecorino. Grana Padano is a fine cheap substitute if you need the cheese as an ingredient in a bigger production. I've also used Berkswell more recently, a British sheep's milk cheese that's based on the same idea as its Italian counterparts: intensely savoury, hard, and easy to grate.

I like to grate Parmesan into soups and sauces; it not only adds depth of flavour but its creaminess gives body and the illusion of thickness. It is especially good with pulses; a handful of grated Parmesan added to a pan of simmering chickpeas, for example, or sprinkled into mashed potato, or in a risotto, or blended into a pesto-style dip (see pages 275–276). Of course, a plate of pasta cries out for a grating of Parmesan or pecorino, and when, after a long night, and in the absence of salt, my friend Joe Woodhouse (a food photographer and former chef) grated a wedge of Parmesan directly into the tomato and chilli pasta sauce he made us for breakfast it delighted an otherwise suffering crowd. I've done the same many times since. (Feta would work well here too.)

When you've grated your cheese all you can and arrive at the rind, don't throw it away, but keep it in foil in the fridge until the day you make a stew or soup. Drop the rind in and

let it roll away in the pan as the contents simmer. You'll never look back.

Lemon

Oranges may not be the only fruit, but were I forced to pick just one, lemons could be. Like all the most useful ingredients, lemon gifts the cook with two distinct but complementary parts: juice and zest. These might both be used in a recipe, but I often find I use them separately, which gives lemons two lives in my kitchen.

I often find that when it is too early to juice a lemon is just when it is perfect to grate it (which inevitably means I have a fruit bowl full of bald lemons). On the flipside, it can be hard to grate a very ripe lemon: a juicy interior can make its zest more elusive. A microplane grater is always useful, and I also like those zesting tools that make pretty yellow shavings. I use lemon zest to add a rounded acidity to the following:

1. On vegetables or salad dishes that are in danger of being too sweet. Baked sweet potato is a fine thing with some lemon zest grated onto it. When I roast squashes – both winter pumpkins and summer courgettes – I like to do so with some fat, generous pieces of lemon rind to add sharp, citric notes.

2. To give thick sauces and dips an acidic kick without changing their consistency (as lemon juice might).

3. In compotes and stewed fruits, when the fruits themselves are very ripe or sweet.

4. One of my favourite recipes from the last couple of years, which also happens to be very easy, is from the *Morito* cookbook. We are instructed to soak little triangles of lemon – rind and flesh – in a bath of water, salt and sugar for a bit, to soften the citrus. Put these on top of some spinach dressed in lemon juice and olive oil.

5. To make things look beautiful! Bright yellow flecks of rind pimp up presentation no end.

To prepare a lemon (or any citrus) for juicing, roll it on a hard surface several times to loosen up the flesh within. Another nice trick is to cut a lemon in half and put it in a frying pan (cut-side down) or under a grill (cut-side up) so that the flesh starts to blacken. This makes it easier to release the juice, which also tastes a little less harsh for being heated. I also use lemon juice for cooking every single day, here's how . . .

1. Green salad needs little more than extra virgin olive oil, lemon juice and salt. If all of the components for this are as good as you can get, you'll have people asking you what your dressing recipe is . . .

2. Another great multi-purpose dressing is simply extra virgin olive oil, lemon juice, a clove of garlic (minced) and three-quarters of a teaspoon of ground cinnamon (see page 260).

3. Filled pasta with sage butter and a squeeze of lemon.

4. In gravy – take the lemon halves from the cavity of your roast chicken and squeeze them out into the meat juices for gravy. This really offsets the fattiness.

5. With fish and fried chicken, always.

6. Squeezed onto avocado that has been mashed onto toast.

7. I don't think I'd ever eat grains like pearl barley, bulgur or quinoa without a lemon to squeeze over them. Lemon juice may well offset richness, but it also adds character to bland, nutty ingredients like these.

8. Squeezed onto boiled broccoli or wilted spinach with a little salt. I eat this practically every day. (This is taken to another level by the Morito lemon peel tip on page 131.)

9. To soak alliums, mainly onions. This softens their texture and counteracts any harshness, but when you add some oil, sugar and salt into the equation, the onions almost caramelise. This is a brilliant trick and would be a great condiment to fish or chicken. I also use it in the salad on pages 112–113.

Extra virgin olive oil

I am always perplexed by recipes that call for 'olive oil for frying' and 'extra virgin olive oil for dressing'. To my mind, the oil in which a recipe is started should be of equal quality to that with which it is finished. The whole point of frying an onion, garlic, or making a soffritto is to develop a sweet, rich and rounded flavour base on which to build. Surely it makes sense for this to taste as good as possible? As is so often the case, the argument for this is often led by money. There are plenty of ways to save money when you shop for food, but I'd suggest not doing so with olive oil. I use extra virgin olive oil for everything and have taken to buying a Tuscan one in 5-litre vats – this lasts at least four months and works out at 25p a day on the ingredient I use most apart from salt. I've done the maths, you do the logic.

I like unfiltered extra virgin olive oils with a greenish colour and peppery flavour. Their opaqueness somehow enhances their mystery and their taste. (Food is, as I have said before, as much an imaginative experience as a tangible one. As Lionel Shriver put it in her novel *Big Brother*, 'More concept than substance, food is the *idea* of satisfaction, far more powerful than satisfaction itself . . .'.)

As well as a base for softening and frying, I use my extra virgin olive oil midway through cooking – I will often glug in extra olive oil as a tomato sauce slow-simmers, for instance – and also leave it on the table for people to put on their own plate or bowl. It sits beside the bowl of salt, and the pepper grinder on our table, the table's trinity. Imagine here a winter stew, or some braised lentils, or a thick soup, with a swirl of extra virgin olive oil and some black pepper.

Cured pork

This I use less than the other seasonings here, mainly because I cook for so many vegetarians. When I want a subtle baseline of smoked meat, I use the likes of bacon, pancetta, chorizo, 'nduja (southern Italian soft spicy sausage) in the early stages of cooking. For example:

1. Throw pancetta into onions sweating or a gently sizzling soffritto base before making a sauce, such as Bolognese, or in my granny's brilliant carrots with bacon recipe (see page 211).

2. A few chunks of chorizo fried up once again with an onion before adding lentils or soaked beans gives the resulting potful Spanish character. (If you want to cheat this and avoid meat, 1 teaspoon of pimentón or hot smoked paprika, gives the illusion of chorizo . . . .)

Women

—— · ——

Anon, who wrote so many poems without signing them, was often a woman.

Virginia Woolf, 'A Room of One's Own'

There is a difference between men's and women's approaches to food . . . Women produce food; men provide food. In other words, we breastfed while the men went out and hunted. Both were necessary.

Margot Henderson, 'Where Are All the Women Chefs?'
in *Lucky Peach*

Our classical tradition has been domestic, with the domestic virtues of quiet enjoyment and generosity.

Jane Grigson, *English Food*

The Italian chef Francesco Mazzei once described his restaurant's food as 'mamma's cooking with chef hats on'. This idea of dressing up the food you were raised with stuck with me. I think – as a general rule – it is the taking of mamma's cooking (and not overly deviating from it) that sets Italian restaurants apart from those based on other cuisines. Italian food is rooted in the home, in the acquired skill and soul of *mammas* and *nonnas* quietly working away in their kitchens to put nourishing, economical family food on the table. More often than not, this isn't an elaborate endeavour. It's a question of making every ingredient, however cheap or lowly, the very best it can be, with knowing flourishes that use everyday things: water, salt, fat.

Like all other skills, cooking is an art improved with practise. And so it follows that it is the people that cook every day who have the greatest chance of mastering it. Historically, that meant women: the great – if unsung – home cooks. Food historian Paula Wolfert once told me that she'd got hold of recipes from Moroccan wives with 'kisses, cuddles and measuring spoons'; in other words, the recipes weren't written down, but had to be passed on orally, coaxed out through friendship and maybe a little flattery. When I decided to write about culinary inheritance and the influence of upbringing on eating, the double meaning of 'mamma' – i.e. my own mother's influence, and the legacy of mamma's (i.e. home) cooking on all food – seemed the ideal title (if you're able to overlook the Spice Girls song of the same name). But as time has worn on, I've wrestled with it.

Is it presumptuous, I've kept asking myself, to assume that everyone's mother did the cooking? Or that people were cooked for at all? Is that what people would think I thought? Does it perpetuate some idea of aproned Mummy in the kitchen and Daddy out at work, or chopping firewood or killing the pig? So, for the record, the title of this book is an innocent play on what I see as the cuisines developed by women in home kitchens, an edible will and testament that is passed down through the generations.

My earliest kitchen memories are with women. Splashing my mum with washing up foam as she tried to clean plates, licking bowls of Granny's coffee cake batter, watching carefully as my aunt Mary tempered caraway seeds in salted butter before adding shredded Savoy cabbage to the distinctive spiced froth, or scissoring curly parsley – finely, very finely – for the creamy sauce to accompany her Christmas Eve gammon. Yes, throughout my life, women have been at the culinary frontline, charging men with the errands (buying stuff they forgot, chopping onions) while conducting an orchestra of kitchen activity.

If a little girl's role model is her mother (or those in maternal roles surrounding her), her inclination will naturally be to grow into their image. I have resisted many of my mother's foibles – like her refusal to buy a salad spinner (oh to grow up and experience dried lettuce!) and love of neon clothing – but she always took charge in the kitchen. We ate from her menus. I too have taken it upon myself to be head chef in every home I have lived since leaving my parents'. I can't bear for food to be an afterthought, or worse, not thought of at all, so my compulsive meal-planning is inflicted on whoever I'm living with at the time.

It never occurred to me that my gender might have something to do with this until I moved in with a partner. We seem to have fallen into an arrangement that I would find irritating were it not so convenient: I am consulted daily about what's for dinner and he sort of tidies up around me (my propensity for clutter means I could never be a chef) and takes on the jobs of which I'm least fond . . . It's a well-oiled machine, but still, sometimes the assumption that I will look after the edible part of our day irks me. Sometimes I imagine myself, long-suffering in a pinafore, dutifully preparing a hearty dinner for my hard-at-work man; a girl from the time before Sisters are Doing it for Themselves, behind the great man, the invisible woman . . . I get into a frenzy of martyrdom, concerned that my love of cooking might segue seamlessly into an expectation that I will always put dinner on the table, and then meander into eventual parenthood, I'll be 'cow heavy and floral' like Sylvia Plath in her maternity nightie, when I will become a faceless caterer to a rabble of little mouths and stomach-liner to a successful husband . . .

What I mean is this: despite the fact that cooking (most of) the food at home is a *choice*, and a process I *love*, it still occasionally presents a tension for me. Is the kitchen always going to be a fraught space for modern women who love to cook?

I don't think it has to, so long as it remains a choice rather than an expectation. When I spoke to Margot Henderson, chef-owner of London's Rochelle Canteen and wife to St John's Fergus, she put it thus: 'When I became a mum, I made beautiful mooshes. Past that, I lost all confidence in my cooking and Fergus would have to cook dinner. That's the thing about motherhood – you lose confidence. You put so much into one thing, the kids, that it's easy to lose yourself. You need to keep something for you.'

Clearly, cooking still gives Margot pleasure. After all, we talk about all this while sitting in her restaurant, Rochelle Canteen – a white-washed old school house in London's Arnold Circus – with pork meatballs (her), an aubergine and chickpea stew (me) and a (possibly second) bottle of chardonnay (us). She doffs her cap to her husband on this, 'Fergus, in all his wisdom, thought that me having my own thing [in Rochelle] would be better for us.' Nevertheless, the point she raises is a valid one. This idea of women becoming obscured by motherhood is a familiar trope, and one of the central themes to Virginia Woolf's 'A Room of One's Own'. Women, she says, need their own sacred space, both for personal sanity and for the feminist cause. For Woolf, this 'room' was her writing. For others, perhaps it is cooking. Whatever that thing is, the message is to find it and cherish it, and to avoid motherhood itself becoming what defines you.

Food was famously important to Woolf. It found its way into many of her novels, not to mention 'A Room of One's Own' itself, in which she famously wrote, 'a good dinner is of great importance to good talk. One cannot think well, love well, sleep well, if one has not dined well'. And yet, for all her enthusiasm towards eating, the preparation of food is implied to be a distraction from woman finding her voice.

And if one asked her, longing to pin down the moment with date and season, but what were you doing on the fifth of April 1868, or the second of November 1875, she would look vague and say that she could remember nothing. For all the dinners are cooked; the plates and cups washed; the children sent to school and gone out into the world. Nothing remains of it all. All has vanished. No biography or history has a word to say about it.

Cooking dinner, washing plates and cups, bringing up the children ... to Woolf, these are duties that have claimed woman when she might have been writing, or making history in any number of ways.

And yet even cooking itself has largely been anonymous. We are left to imagine faces and names for so many women cooks that worked in the kitchens of previous centuries; there's a whole *baterie* of recipes whose history remains foggy. Could the quote at the beginning of this chapter refer just as easily to recipes as poems? ('Anon, who wrote so many poems without signing them, was often a woman.')

Not yet being a parent, I haven't experienced the sense of vanishing that new mothers are said sometimes to feel, but I do know that – woman or man, old or young, with or without children – it's important to have and treasure a pastime that is your own. For many, including me, this is cooking. I love to cook because it is an everyday opportunity to create, and because I relish holding onto the reins of my personal wellbeing, and because it is the route to a meal time. Cooking is, after all, the very best way of knowing exactly what you're fuelling your body with, from the source of your ingredients to how you've handled them. What's more, whether I'm alone, quietly stirring a risotto while the radio hums, or cooking with someone else, talking, probably drinking wine, making food – for myself or for others – is something that I love to do. Why should the loaded matter of my sex get in the way of that?

Among those who cook, there remains a schism between notions of 'cook' and 'chef'. Implicit in each of these words is still a suggestion of sex. Despite how many talented female chefs are working today – April Bloomfield, Margot Henderson, Gabrielle Hamilton, just to name three I admire – the word 'chef' still woefully suggests a bloke in a big white hat, while 'cook' assumes a more domestic humility. One thing's for sure, though. Unassuming home-cooked food has never been more popular, and perhaps now more than ever, books written by cooks whose only training ground has been the home kitchen are gaining traction.

When I talked with Jamie Oliver, he spoke of his first ever TV series, *The Naked Chef,* thus, 'It was more political than I realised. When I started [in the late nineties], cooking was a thing for girls, and by the time I was a finished, it got you the girls. Now I almost think men cook more than women.' I do feel we are finally getting to a place where cooking can be viewed as open to either sex — not disempowering for women or emasculating for men, just a resourceful way of knowing how to take care of yourself.

I do hope we don't go so far as to muddy the differences between male and female cooking entirely though. Because we are different, that needs to be celebrated, in the kitchen as much as anywhere else.

Anna Del Conte

The first time I went to lunch with Anna Del Conte was the Monday after a particularly long session in the pub. I'd decided to have a gentle week.

But then I got to Anna's in Shaftesbury at 11.30am and she asked me if I wanted a sherry and, in a move that testifies to my complete lack of self-control, I responded, 'Um, are you having one?', to which Anna said, 'Of course!' So I started my week of good behaviour with a manzanilla. And progressed on to red wine.

The second time I went to lunch with Anna Del Conte, I knew better than to try not to drink and took with me a bottle of Gavi di Gavi at train temperature. This served the double purpose of cooking liquor for clams (destined for *spaghetti alle vongole*) and the liquid with which to wash it all down. Anna suggested I pour us both a glass, and I apologised for it being warm. Anna looked at me blankly, then said, 'I don't care, I'm not French.' So I duly poured us both some warm Gavi, the temperature of which felt fitting for the weather; outside, rain poured down over Dorset's Blackmoor Vale – the verdant, almost buxom, view from Anna's kitchen window.

Anna drinks, very moderately, with every meal (except breakfast, I assume). She also smokes two cigarettes a day – one after lunch and before her nap, the other before bed, cannot fathom finishing a meal without fruit, and prefers eating two or three small courses to eating a lot of the same thing. She is a creature of habit, 'like everyone', she says, and also very Italian, despite some seventy years on British soil. She is also 91, impossibly glamorous, travels often, lives independently in a house next door to her daughter Julia, and had read all four of Elena Ferrante's Neapolitan novels when I'd only just heard about the first.

From what I can tell, Anna's habits are written into her like code. Especially regarding cooking, eating and drinking. She carries herself around her kitchen with the grace of someone who has done it all their life, who knows the territory like the back of their hand (she will only cook in her own kitchen), and doesn't stop naturally to think about what she is doing – she just does it. Having made a career out of writing recipes and imparting kitchen know-how to English readers, there is an irony to this. She doesn't like having her flow interrupted with questions about quantities of this or that, or why she's doing a certain thing. I ask her how much chilli has gone into the *vongole*, which receives another sort of blank look and 'I haven't the foggiest idea, I'm sorry.' Despite having adapted and translated hundreds of Italian recipes for British households in her time – her cookbook career started in her fifties with a book about pasta, followed by adapting US-based food writer Marcella Hazan's books about Italian cooking for the UK market – it strikes me that one of the things Anna Del Conte most likes about cooking is the not needing to translate, the absence of language.

Del Conte was born in Milan in 1925, the daughter of a stock-broker. Before war broke out, she remembers having a cook at home, Maria, 'my friend', she says – Anna easily forges friendships over a work surface, I discover. She'd observe Maria like a hawk as she went about her kitchen work. In the introduction to *Amaretto, Apple Cake and Artichokes: The Best of Anna Del Conte*, she writes: 'As she worked, Maria sang the Communist songs that were forbidden during the Fascist years, while I watched, fascinated . . . by her dexterity in flicking potato gnocchi down the prongs of a fork. It was listening to her discussing with my mother what to do with the mountain of *porcini* on the kitchen table, or pointing out how the beautiful slices of *prosciutto di Parma* had just the right amount of fat around them that laid the foundations of my knowledge of cooking.' Mamma's cooking, then, but from another mamma.

Anna is also wistful about Maria's supreme *polpette* (meatballs), which, during the autumn, she'd lace with truffle, a princely addition to a pauper's meal. This could only ever have happened in the famously truffle-growing north of Italy. Anna speaks of her Lombardian homeland's culinary riches, 'Even during the war, we ate very well at home. We were lucky. People all over the country were starving but around Milan the land is very fertile, so we had everything: grapes, cows, pigs, chickens, vegetables . . . everything except olive oil.' This emphasis on Italian regional nuances is important to Anna; in 1987, she was the first to detail the ingredients, recipes and traditions of the twenty regions in her book *Gastronomy of Italy*. What might then have seemed superfluous information to its British readership was and is absolutely essential, not to mention intuitive, to any Italian cook. Like the appetite for tougher pasta the further south in the country you travel (Anna proclaims the spaghetti she cooks for our *vongole* 'perfect for

me as a Milanese, but a Neapolitan would call it over-cooked'),
or how a tomato sauce reflects the territory from whence it
came, with olive oil and garlic in the south, and butter and
onion in the north.

Such sound bites (which they are, quite literally) roll off Del
Conte's tongue like a lick of a gelato, as automatic as they are
moreish. Pasta water should 'taste like the Mediterranean, not
the Atlantic' (because it is saltier), and 'what you leave out of
Italian food is as important as what you leave in' (like the removal
of garlic from frying oil, or the *spaghetti alle vongole* without
tomatoes which is, in her mind, superior for its simplicity).
'I never used a recipe book, except Artusi,* it all came very
naturally,' she says, although clearly the learning started early
with Maria and, from the war onwards ('with which we lost all
our money'), her mother. Mamma Del Conte was a patient cook,
excelling at *risotti, cassola* (Italian cassoulet with beans), and –
her speciality – *arrosto all'acqua*, a cut of beef 'roast in water'
with only a little salt and rosemary, beside which she would stay
for an hour and a half, mothering the pot on the stove, feeding it
water, tablespoon by tablespoon, very slowly.

Cooking on the hob is Del Conte's preference, something
she inherited not just from her mother, but many an Italian
mamma and *nonna* before her. 'I like to watch and smell as I'm
cooking.' She explains how the likes of French beans are done
boiling when you can smell them, and goes on to say that,
traditionally, because keeping the house cool was a priority, the
majority of Italian kitchens wouldn't have had ovens. The local
baker's oven provided for a community when one was called

---

* Pellegrino Artusi was a 19th century Italian writer and author of *Science in the
Kitchen and the Art of Eating Well.*

for, but otherwise it was up to the stovetop or home-kindled fires to provide heat and bring together the elements of a meal. 'My mother had an extremely fine nose and palate. I remember when she was quite old, about my age now, and my son had stirred a pot of something she was cooking while she was out of the room. She knew instantly, by smell and by sense.' The preparation of food is a sensory thing, then, picked up by Del Conte via nature and nurture, and tapping into the most basic of instincts.

Nature is a theme in Italian cooking, but I think for Anna Del Conte especially. Britain greeted her in 1949 with what she calls 'a sad story', which got only sadder in the sixties as raw ingredients became industrialised. Having met an Englishman, her late husband Oliver Waley, and had three children here, Anna was left to make the best of a bad situation. Tomatoes looked anaemic, bread brimmed with additives (in 1961 the Chorleywood process was introduced to industrialise bread production), and olive oil was nigh-on impossible to find. The exception to this was London's Soho, of course, where Anna – a west London resident – could get what she considered to be the most basic Italian provisions. 'Even in the fifties, when there were still rations, you could find everything in Soho. There was a French butcher who sold brain, sweetbreads, the stuff the British wouldn't eat. I was able to find aubergine and pepper there too. This was all at a time when you could park in Soho, of course.' Clearly she has lived a privileged life; but in the abundant Britain I have always known, it's curious to think of red peppers as a luxury. Like Claudia Roden (page 23), Anna found ways of negotiating her native appetites in her adoptive home, 'I learned to put little extras of things – salt, butter, oil – into dishes to compensate for inferior ingredients.'

This kind of experimentation has not only helped British home cooks to emulate the plates of holidays past, it's also encouraged Anna to innovate in her own cooking. Much as there are rules in Italian cuisine, rules to which she subscribes, I get the impression that Anna has relaxed her views on some of these over the years. Namely, her disdain for what she has often described as 'Britalian' cooking, the British way of mimicking Italian food with too many ingredients and flavours that are unsubtle, too strong. 'I'm traditional, but less purist now,' she says. Recipes like pasta with Marmite (page 77), and another pasta dish she makes with finely chopped leeks and curry powder (pasta's answer to Coronation chicken?) demonstrate a mellower approach to kitchen orthodoxy, the peaceful (and delicious) coexistence of Britain and Italy on the table.

In 2016, I asked Anna to write a piece entitled 'The 10 Commandments of Italian Cooking'. Fearing the premise too rigid, she was worried about taking on such a headline, but went ahead with an article whose advice included finding good quality ingredients, seasoning as you go, not putting Parmesan on fish, and eating pasta and risotto without accompaniment. Her introduction tempered the suggested dogmatism of its title: 'You will not go to hell if you do not follow [these Commandments], nor to heaven if you do – though the result of your efforts may send you there, granted. Here they are: not on two tablets, but just a piece of newspaper.'

A major departure from purism has come more recently in the form of *FreeFrom all'Italiana*, a pocket guide to cooking Italian food well without gluten and dairy. She resisted taking on a project that inevitably excluded her 'beloved' wheat pasta until she tried some – pleasantly surprising – alternatives. When we meet, Anna is in the midst of recipe testing and has an archive of gluten-free pastas exploding from her cupboards: rice penne and maize fusilli, black bean spaghetti, some shapes I can't identify made with mung and edamame beans. At 91, she could well have drawn the line at branching out into such dubious territory as the exclusion of whole food groups. But I know by now that she relishes a challenge.

Today though, back at her Dorset table, we're sticking to a classic. There's space for purism and defiance here. Her attitudes to the rules have relaxed, as have mine to drinking on a Monday (rather quickly). In their Gavi-filled sauna, the clams too have loosened up, now open in their shells and laid bare. Together, we sit down to eat them, laced with oil, garlic and parsley, and tossed through good old-fashioned spaghetti.

Potatoes

— ✿ —

The canteen staff stopped asking me what I wanted after a while. It always went the same: jacket potato with cottage cheese, please, yeah and some salad too, thanks (iceberg, cucumber, cress, that triumvirate of the cafeteria garnish). The potato was distinct: skin baggy, not crispy. I guiltily enjoyed the potato like this, not for its skin – that's always better crispy – but because the over-cooked flesh within had taken on that sweet, yellowing, buttery quality that baked potatoes assume when cooked and then reheated.

This daily plateful in the Leeds University student union during the winter of 2004 offered me deep, uninspired comfort. I felt dislocated and very alone in that first term. Everything that my London life identified about me felt a long way away, and my ritual of going to the union for lunch and doing the crossword between lectures offered a small touchstone for home.

Most of those days blur into one now, but I remember one in particular because it was the day when, over an over-cooked baked potato, I met my best friend. As usual, the other Freshers bustled around me, catching up on last night's antics. As usual, the union smelled of lager and bleach stamped into the floor. As usual at that time, the Shapeshifters were probably playing on the radio. As usual, I was negotiating the crossword while,

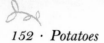

as usual, I scooped cottage cheese and jaundiced spud flesh from its jacket.

'Mina!' I looked up, mouth full. I couldn't place her. 'Sophie, from the audition.'

Ah yes. The last time I'd seen this girl – a girl I'd never actually met – I'd been half-heartedly shouting 'cunt' over and over. Everything I did in that first term I did ambivalently (except for ordering a baked potato with cottage cheese and salad for lunch). My mum had encouraged me to get into a student theatre group and I'd gone to audition for *The Vagina Monologues*. I hadn't got in. I really didn't want to talk to this girl about my ineffectual expletive shouting, and I didn't want her to watch me eating my potato.

But, in a move that would be echoed so many times over the subsequent years, Sophie took one look at what I was eating and went to get herself exactly the same thing.

It's funny how perspectives on these things differ. I felt rather lame in her eyes, a monotonous eater, a lonely crossworder and an unsuccessful actress. She says she took one look at me and decided she wanted to be my friend. Knowing now how much she loves a baked potato, it may well have been that which seduced her. But over that lunch, I made my first new friend at university. And now she's an old friend, and I have potatoes to thank. Had she not ordered herself one, had we not eaten that meal together, and bonded over the sad absence of Branston pickle with which to load the limp skins, we'd arguably never have gone on to eat so many baked potatoes together – all over the world, from Berkeley to Belize to Brixton – for the next decade. Sophie and I owe a lot to potatoes. And these days we always make sure the skins are crispy.

* * *

The potato's presence in the Western home has been fairly constant since the 18th century.* We have relied upon the humble tuber's ability to pad out meals cost-effectively, but perhaps not given it the love it has deserved. Too often, we depend on the potato's presence at a meal but neglect to praise it, preferring instead to compliment the meat or the sauce or another vegetable, perhaps one with the novelty factor of a more fleeting season. If I were a potato I'd be pretty pissed off.

Virginia Woolf called the triptych arrangement of meat, potatoes and a vegetable on one's plate a 'homely trinity', but to you and me it's known less elegantly as 'meat and two veg'. One of the 'veg' in said arrangement is always potatoes – unlike the second veg, or indeed the meat, which could change from one day to the next – while potatoes remain the faithful constant. Potatoes probably feel like the Supremes must have felt while Diana Ross was busy taking the limelight. What a bum deal.

That said, you hear about it when there's something *not right* with the potatoes. For such well-loved, familiar and reassuringly bland ingredients, they can be curiously divisive. Everyone has an opinion about them. I've known families feud about whether to roast in olive oil or duck fat. I've known my own father skip meals because the potatoes have been roasted, not baked. I've known otherwise wonderful restaurant meals ruined for my boyfriend because the potatoes weren't up to scratch.

Potatoes are easy to grow, cheap to buy and versatile ingredients, which goes a long way to explain not only their ubiquity, but also the reason why they're easily upstaged by

* In *A History of Food in 100 Recipes*, William Sitwell charts the potato's progress in Europe from its discovery in the New World in the 16th century to its eventual acceptance in British kitchens.

more expensive ingredients – namely meat. As Elizabeth David had it in *French Country Cooking*, it wasn't difficult for spuds to be upstaged by other ingredients because so many housewives were clueless about what to do with them: 'In our own day we have witnessed the enraged British housewife, backed up by an indignant press, deprived of her national birthright, obliged to queue for a pound or two of potatoes. Too well we know to what base uses those potatoes were put. Boiled to ruins on the outside, and hard within, battered to a grey pulp by a blunt instrument, interspersed with lumps like a boarding-house mattress.' Poor potatoes: as though the assumption of their availability – rain, shine, war or peace (potato rationing started in 1947 after a terrible winter's frost destroyed crops) – weren't bad enough, then they are to be abused in the kitchen too.

In fact, boiling potatoes 'to ruins' – in other words, boiling them almost to smithereens – is the secret to roast potatoes in my house. I spent years peering over the stove trying to gauge the point of optimal parboiling, before realising that I didn't need the 'par' prefix at all. The fluff that develops on 'over-boiled' potatoes combines with fat – I always use olive oil – to form a coat of unrivalled crispiness, protecting the gloriously soft, salted starch within.

FREDDIE'S
ROAST POTATOES

It's better to use floury potatoes here. When over-boiled, they develop the fluff that makes for the crispiness of dreams. For the bashed variety, use new potatoes and bash them with the back of a wooden spoon once boiled.

———

1kg potatoes, cut into quarters

6 tbsp extra virgin olive oil

salt

———

1. Preheat the oven to 220°C/425°F/Gas mark 7. Put the potatoes in a large saucepan, cover with cold water and season generously with salt. Place over a medium–high heat, bring to the boil and cook for around 30 minutes, or until they are soft, yield easily to a knife and are starting to become fluffy. Drain. If your potatoes are really falling apart, it's worth letting them dry out slightly before adding the olive oil.

2. Transfer the potatoes to a large baking tray. Coat in the olive oil and roast in the oven for 40 minutes, tossing them 2 or 3 times during cooking to brown them evenly. Cook until they are golden and crisp. Sprinkle with salt and serve.

Now, many would disagree with this carry-on. I see it as a good example of negotiating tradition for yourself. Cooking is a question of trial and error to find the way that you like doing things best. Here are my observations on potato prep:

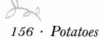

1. Potatoes are starchy. The removal of starch makes them go more crispy, so if you are making roast potatoes or potato chips, wash your cut potatoes thoroughly before roasting – several times. If you're washing your potatoes anyway, then I also think it makes sense to buy muddy ones. Why not? It's worth reminding ourselves where they come from – they are 'earth apples' (*pommes de terre* in French), after all.

2. The starch in potatoes also makes them less absorbent of salt. It's therefore important to be generous with salt when you're boiling potatoes – you want the water to taste almost briney, like when you're boiling pasta.

3. To test when a boiled potato is done (assuming you're not over-boiling for roasties), take a sharp knife and prick a potato. If the potato slips slowly off the knife and tumbles back into the water, your spuds are ready to eat.

4. I've always been confused, irritated even, by recipes that call for 'waxy' or 'floury' potatoes, as though we are to know one from the other when we're in the grocery store. As a rule, waxy potatoes – like Charlotte, Desiree and Pink Fir – hold their shape beautifully so suit being boiled or put to work in salads. Floury potatoes have that fall-apart quality I look for in my roast potatoes, and are ideal for mashes and baking – the Maris Piper is a mainstream example of a floury spud, but others include Golden Wonder and Pentland Squire. If you're in any doubt about whether a variety is waxy or floury, then go for an all-rounder like Cara, King Edward or Maris Piper.

Potatoes need little more than salt and fat, and perhaps on occasion something aromatic – rosemary, some spice – to be one of the best things there is to eat. For this reason, recipes are inessential; true to most of my cooking, potato meals revolve more around a set of ideas than a rubric. Here are the things we do most with potatoes at home:

1. The arrival of new potatoes – like Jersey Royals (the best known variety, but also Pentland Javelin, Arran Pilot, Maris Bard and Ulster Sceptre – don't potatoes have the best names?) – is an annual treat. Few things say 'home comfort' like the scent of new potatoes simmering gently in salted water with a sprig of mint – that's aromatherapy for you after a cold winter's eating. Serve with butter and a little salt if necessary (remember to boil them with plenty of salt, which means you won't need much – if any – salt to serve). I'm also partial to a dusting of white pepper.

2. Baked potatoes are doubtless better with crispy skins – if done properly I'm pretty sure they're unbeatable. Make sure your oven is nice and hot to ensure said crispiness – around 200°C/400°F/Gas mark 6 – and don't forget to prick the spuds beforehand. Again, it's hard to beat butter here (and Branston pickle), but I like to make a garlicky yoghurt with five tablespoons of natural yoghurt, a pinch of salt, black pepper and a small grated garlic clove. You could further elevate this into something resembling a tzatziki with some grated cucumber or carrot and a dash of olive oil. Twice-baked potatoes are usually the happy upshot of baked potatoes not being eaten the first time around. Reheated in the oven a second time, the potato flesh takes on the yellowish, more toasted quality like the over-cooked potatoes that Leeds Uni

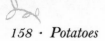

union had. You could also mix the inside with some butter, cheese, spring onion and parsley, then re-fill the skins, put them back in the oven for 10 minutes – an excellent meal with a simple green salad.

3. Tortilla is a serious business in my house. About a kilogram of potatoes (preferably waxy ones with a nice red skin, like Desiree, as you want them to be fairly robust and to hold their shape) are peeled and cut thinly into half moons. We deep-fry them in butter with one finely sliced onion, then pat them dry of excess fat. We then beat six eggs, season them generously with salt, and mix the potatoes and onion into the egg before frying them over a medium–high heat in a small pan (size of pan is crucial to a tortilla with even consistency). Flip after 5 minutes and leave to cook for a further 3 minutes. Delicious hot but even better cold, in a sandwich.

4. Everyone has their own way of doing mash. I like butter, whole milk, salt and nutmeg. It always pays to make double of this simplest of preparations so you have the wherewithal for fishcakes or a pie the following day. A superior mash has a generous spoonful each of Dijon and wholegrain mustard. I'm also fond of mixing another boiled root vegetable into my mash – turnips are delicious, as is celeriac or swede. Instead of milk or cream, try yoghurt. The slight sourness works well with wholegrain mustard especially. I like to turn leftover mash into a soft bed for baked eggs (like the baked eggs and mashed celeriac recipe on pages 39–40) or into croquettes.

5. We eat a lot of roast potatoes (which I realise bodes poorly for my cardiac health). We also have them fried and in salads fairly often – again, these feature in the recipes that follow,

the dressings and sauces that accompany them are an easy way of advancing something as humble as the potato into a veritable luxury.

ROSEMARY POTATOES

One of my favourite things to eat.

———

SERVES 2–4

1kg potatoes, cut into 1cm dice (unpeeled)

2 tbsp extra virgin olive oil

4 sprigs of rosemary, needles only, finely chopped

5 garlic cloves, bashed

salt

———

1. Bring a pan of generously salted water to the boil, then add the diced potatoes.

2. While the potatoes are cooking, heat the oil in a large frying pan over a low heat and add the rosemary and garlic. Fry gently for a few minutes, to allow the oil to become infused with the flavours of the rosemary and garlic.

3. Check the potatoes are cooked by prodding them with a knife. If they slide off the knife, they're ready. Drain them well, then add them to the oil in the pan. Make sure each piece of potato glistens

with oil, then increase the heat and fry, stirring, until they take on a burnished golden crispiness. Season with salt to taste and serve, perhaps with brava sauce (pages 282–283), or something else dunk-worthy.

THE POTATO SALAD

. . . is a concept on which people seem to agree. The simple combination of sweet, new season potatoes and mayonnaise is enough in itself, even better with a big scoop of Dijon mustard, better still with the addition of wholegrain mustard, reaching dizzy heights with some chopped up gherkin, capers, dill or parsley. Like *salsa verde* and tomato sauce, the potato salad is an imprecise art almost guaranteed to be delicious.

CORONATION POTATOES WITH ALMONDS AND QUICK PICKLED RADISHES

The potato salad's answer to Coronation chicken.

———

SERVES 4

500g new potatoes, cut into roughly 3cm cubes

2 tbsp mayonnaise

2 tbsp natural yoghurt

1 heaped tsp mild curry powder

salt

bunch of spring onions, roughly chopped

handful of flaked almonds, lightly toasted

coriander, chopped, to serve (optional)

For the quick pickled radish

big bunch of radishes, very thinly sliced

4 tbsp white wine vinegar

4 tbsp caster sugar

juice of ½ lemon

big pinch of salt

½ tsp ground turmeric

———

1. Cook the potatoes in a saucepan of generously salted boiling water for about 10 minutes, until cooked through, but still holding their shape robustly. Drain and transfer to a serving bowl.

2. Combine the radish with the remaining pickle ingredients in a bowl, and leave to pickle for 15 minutes to 1 hour.

3. Mix the mayonnaise, yoghurt and curry powder together, season with salt, then fold into the potatoes with the spring onions.

4. Scatter with the toasted almonds, then arrange the pickled radishes on top, and scatter with coriander, if using.

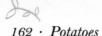

BOULANGERE POTATOES

This was named for the bakeries in France where home cooks would take their roasting trays brimming with the spuddy/stocky mix ready to be cooked. It isn't a dish I grew up with, but I really like it. It occupies a space between dauphinoise and a more innocent tray bake of roasted vegetables. It's hard to improve on a combination of potatoes sweetened with onions, herbs, seasoning and a little butter; you get a lot of good flavour without lots of oil or cream, which is probably part of the reason it makes such a regular appearance on my table.

SERVES 4

1.5kg potatoes, peeled and thinly sliced

2 white onions, thinly sliced into half moons

leaves from a bunch of thyme and/or rosemary,
rubbed gently to release their flavour

350ml vegetable or chicken stock

a few knobs of butter

salt and black pepper

---

1. Preheat the oven to 190°C/375°F/Gas mark 5.

2. Arrange the thinly sliced potatoes in a deep roasting tray – the kind in which you would cook a chicken – layering them with the onions, herbs, salt and pepper and reserving the potato slices that are most pleasing to look at for the top layer.

3. Pour the stock over the potatoes, sprinkle with more salt and pepper and dot little knobs of butter all over the top.

4. Put the tray in the oven and cook for about 1 hour, until the potatoes are golden on top and cooked through (you should be able to insert a sharp knife without resistance). This makes a good side for almost anything, but is equally king with a mountain of green salad – fresh and filling.

POTATO, TALEGGIO AND ROSEMARY QUICHE

When I was little, we often had a meal called 'bits and pieces'. Conveniently, this created an occasion out of 'hoovering up' – as my dad always puts it – recent leftovers, wilting salady things, and Edam cheese past its best (a childhood staple, of which Dad remains very fond, that he deftly slid from its red rubbery skin and tidied up into dice). This has continued into the present day and is what my parents still do for Saturday lunch: a medley of cold cuts and reheated stuff – my father's favourite kind of meal, full of opportunities for chutney and hot sauce and Marmite, on everything, together. *Now, this might sometimes involve leftover quiche. It might also involve leftover ingredients that could go into a quiche. From April through to early summer, I often have cold boiled new potatoes from a previous meal, which here I have added to my friend Oliver Rowe's brilliantly versatile base recipe for quiche, along with some rather tired, so lightly fried, spring onions, chopped rosemary needles, and Taleggio cheese (all interchangeable for alternatives). With the right flavours (good cheese, a hit of lemon,*

a herb), spuds in quiche make for a really complete meal alongside salad. You'll enjoy hoovering it up hot and fresh from the oven or as cold leftovers.

———

MAKES 1 LARGE QUICHE

For the pastry

225g cold unsalted butter, cubed, plus extra for greasing

450g plain flour, plus extra for dusting

3 eggs

tiny dash of milk

For the filling

500g new potatoes (preferably Jersey Royals – use leftover cooked potatoes if you have some to hand)

extra virgin olive oil, for frying

bunch of spring onions

3 sprigs of rosemary

2 garlic cloves, finely chopped

4 eggs, lightly beaten

200ml double cream

200g crème fraiche

1 tbsp mustard (Dijon or wholegrain)

grated zest of ½ unwaxed lemon

100g Taleggio, 75g grated and 25g sliced

50g Parmesan, grated

100g asparagus tips, steamed or boiled, chopped into 2cm pieces

———

1. First make the pastry. Rub the butter and flour together with the tips of your fingers until the mixture reaches the consistency of breadcrumbs. Beat 2 of the eggs, add them to the mixture, and incorporate only just until the pastry comes together in a ball. Press into a thick disc, wrap in cling film and refrigerate for at least 1 hour.

2. Grease a 30cm tart tin (the kind with a detachable base) with butter. Remove the dough from the fridge and leave for 15 minutes, then unwrap and, on a lightly floured surface, roll into a 4mm-thick disc a bit larger than the tart tin. Drape the pastry over the tin, gently push it into the edges and let it hang over the rim and nearly touch the work surface. Working round with your fingers, bring the overhang back into the tin, pressing it into the sides and corners to create a double layer. The pastry should be slightly higher than the edge of the tin to allow for shrinkage. Prick the bottom with the prongs of a fork, and place back in the fridge. Preheat the oven to 180°C/350°F/Gas mark 4.

3. Line the chilled pastry case with crumpled baking parchment and fill with baking beans – make sure you use lots to really weigh down the pastry and hold it in position. Bake in the oven until the pastry is starting to colour around the edges. Remove the paper and beans, then return to the oven until the pastry is golden. Beat the remaining egg and dash of milk together and brush this all over the pastry. Return to the oven until the egg is cooked and glossy. Remove from the oven and leave to cool before filling.

4. Reduce the oven temperature to 170°C/325°F/Gas mark 3½. If you don't have any leftover potatoes, boil a batch, then cool. Cut the potatoes into 0.5cm-thick slices.

5. Heat a glug of olive oil in a frying pan, then add the spring onions, rosemary and garlic and fry gently for a few minutes until softened and fragrant.

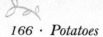

6. Combine the eggs, cream, crème fraiche, mustard, lemon zest, grated cheeses, spring onions, herbs, garlic and potatoes in a bowl. Pour into the pastry case, arranging the asparagus tips on top, then sprinkle the top with the Taleggio slices. Cook in the middle of the oven for about 25 minutes until just starting to rise and colour. Don't let it cook too much or the egg mixture will split. Remove from the oven and leave to cool before serving. I like mine at room temperature as the egg and pastry are at their best like this, but some prefer it warmer.

RACHEL RODDY'S PASTA AND POTATOES (PASTA E PATATE)

At first, putting two carbs together in one dish made no sense to me, but such is my devotion to both pasta and potatoes, I decided it had to be worth a try. Thank goodness for such clarity of thought.

—

SERVES 4

6 tbsp extra virgin olive oil, plus extra for drizzling

1 onion, diced

1 carrot, diced

1 celery stick, diced

2 bay leaves or a sprig of rosemary

600g (about 2 medium) potatoes (of any kind),
peeled and cut into chunks

1.4 litres water or light stock (such as chicken or vegetable)

170g pasta (quadrucci, pastina, farfalle, or broken spaghetti)

pecorino or Parmesan, grated, to serve

salt and black pepper

———

1. Heat the olive oil in a heavy-based saucepan over a low–medium heat, then add the onion, carrot and celery, along with a pinch of salt, and fry gently until soft and translucent. Add the bay leaves or rosemary and the potatoes and fry, stirring so each cube is coated with oil for a couple more minutes.

2. Add the water or stock and another small pinch of salt, bring to a lively simmer, then reduce to a gentle simmer for 15 minutes, or until the potato is very soft and breaks up slightly if pressed with the back of a wooden spoon. Add the pasta, increase the heat slightly and cook for a further 10 minutes or so or until the pasta is cooked, stirring and adding a little more water if it looks to be getting too thick. Check the seasoning (remembering you are going to add salty cheese) and grind over some black pepper. Serve with grated pecorino or Parmesan stirred in, or simply a streak of olive oil.

POTATO,
RED PEPPER AND
OLIVE OIL STEW

The flavours in this stew were inspired by Spain – wine, garlic, olive oil, pimentón. The challenge is to get the potatoes to fully absorb all the flavours surrounding them. I find the key to this is making it the day or morning before you intend to eat it.

SERVES 4

10 tbsp extra virgin olive oil

1 onion, roughly chopped

4 garlic cloves, roughly chopped

4 red peppers, seeded and cut into strips

500g waxy potatoes, cut into roughly 1 x 2cm chunks

1 x 400g tin of whole plum tomatoes

1 small glass of white wine

2 small glasses of water

1 bay leaf

pinch of pimentón

squeeze of lemon juice

salt and black pepper

----

1. Heat 6 tablespoons of the olive oil in a heavy-based saucepan over a low–medium heat, then add the onion and lightly sauté for a couple of minutes before adding the garlic. Allow them to cook together, gently, for a couple more minutes.

2. Add the peppers, coating each strip with a film of the olive oil, then cover and leave to cook for 10–15 minutes.

3. Add the potatoes, tinned tomatoes, wine, water, bay leaf, pimentón, lemon juice and 2 tablespoons of the olive oil to the pan, stir, and season generously with salt and pepper. Replace the lid and let it bubble away over a medium heat for a good 30 minutes, stirring occasionally. After 30 minutes, lower the heat a bit, cock the lid, and simmer for a further 30 minutes.

4. Test the potatoes – they may need a little longer. If they do, add some more water (or wine – why not?), or bash some or all of the potatoes so that they take on the sauce as they cook more.

5. I think this is best left overnight, then reheated to eat the following day. When you do so, make sure there's crusty bread at the ready. Serve with yoghurt, if that appeals.

Eating meat

——— . ———

Being a vegetarian should not automatically mean a denial of pleasurable foods, or an acceptance of unpalatable ones.

Annie Bell, *Evergreen*

I believe that life is taken at every step, whether killing a cow or harvesting grain. I don't believe in a pure place, and I think it naïve to think there is one.

Deborah Madison, interviewed in January 2016

Mortadella was to blame. Every time I resolved to stop eating meat, I'd get to the Sainsbury's charcuterie counter with Mum on a Saturday morning, and mortadella would present itself: fat-dappled, pistachio-flecked, obscenely pink.

For both of us, mortadella has always been a weakness. As a ten-year-old, I found it impossible to resist this most favourite of cold cuts on a Saturday lunchtime – that wonderful spread, so rich in its sparseness, of good bread, cheese, sliced tomatoes, chutney and the bowled, cold remains of whatever we'd eaten the night before.

I did eventually manage it, however. The frolicking lambs and peaceful cows and mud-bathing pigs in my mind's eye prevailed and I stopped eating meat in 1995. My tempestuous social life (oh, girls' schools . . .) meant it felt particularly inconsistent

to eat those I considered to be my real friends in the world: animals. I wasn't so zealous to include fish in my list of friends, but at least I felt better for saving my fellow land mammals from my plate. This sometimes prompted questions – 'what makes a cow's life more important than a fish's?' etc. – and, I admit, I hadn't really thought that through. I just did what felt right to me. This was partly based on example – my mum, similarly, was selective (she eats fish and very occasionally snaffles a piece of ham when she likes the look of it, but not much else) – and partly because I *did* identify more with cows than with fish. Their suffering felt more real in my childish imagination. Plus I liked fish more than I liked beef. At the age of ten, this all made perfect sense.

Though my eating habits have changed since then, I stand by my decision in the face of aggressive questioning about meat-eating. I think the use of 'vegetarian' as a blanket term that refers to various approaches to meat and fish exclusion is waning, and I agree that it is inaccurate to label yourself as a vegetarian if you eat fish. But it was a label which, at one time, enabled me to listen to my instincts and select how I ate based on them – a defence mechanism, perhaps. To this day, I don't want to eat fish or meat just because it's there, slapped on my plate; it should be a celebration of being *able* to eat it, of the life that animal has given to good cooking.

When I returned to eating meat, mortadella wasn't actually responsible. It was the summer of 2006 and it was chicken drumsticks, hissing as they blackened on a barbecue, that seduced me back to the flesh. The notion of eating meat again had been bizarre, anathema even, until that point, but in the event it was an effortless and happy reunion. It was the summer before I moved to northern California where, more than anywhere else I've been, you are encouraged to source food consciously and to revel in this choice. Over the course of the year, I felt my way back into the realm of eating chicken with something like a hangover. It was a rollercoaster; waves of elation on eating it, and afterwards of guilt, a bit like how Shakespeare seemed to feel about sex: 'a bliss in proof, and proved, a very woe'.

Nowadays, I don't call myself vegetarian or pescatarian, but I am selective about the meat and fish that I eat. Good, organic examples of both aren't cheap, and the only way around this is to eat them less often. A typical week for me is meat-free throughout except for the occasional roast chicken on Sunday and something that puts its leftovers and stock to work the next day. I can go for weeks without eating fish, save for the modest addition of anchovy fillets here and there for flavour (see pages 127–128).

So, I am mainly vegetarian. This may not be a widely accepted label, but there's arguably too much emphasis on putting a name to things, on identifying as veggie or vegan or this or that, and not enough on every person's own decisions about what they do and don't eat. The most pertinent decision, it seems to me, is between a dichotomy cited by Sandra M. Gilbert in *The Culinary Imagination*: '. . . in the industrialised world we have come to inhabit a culinary landscape marked by the dichotomy between "whole" ("slow", "real") food and technologically produced "fast" food . . . .' There is a huge difference between animals kept in cramped conditions, that never see daylight, which are separated from their animal peers, and eat mass-produced feed, and those that roam and graze freely together. And, given that the best sustainable agriculture involves animals and plants working in tandem – the plants feed the animals, the animals then give

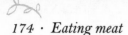

back to the plants, and round and round it goes – I believe it's important to support this system. It's a system that works, that holds creatures and land in balance, and if it's done as ethically as possible, it is a good thing.

The argument is less 'should I eat meat or not?' than 'what meat should I eat and not eat?' The message is basic, and recalls Alice Waters (see page 85): know where your food has come from, and cook with it from scratch. And, as Deborah Madison said to me (see page 180), 'it can be more complex to take the middle of the road argument. Nothing wants to die, we know that.' These observations tap into a universal truth, that humans are omnivores (with, as Michael Pollan titled his book,* a 'dilemma'), which assumes us a diet of animals and plants. That doesn't mean you have to eat both. And it is sensible to eat more plants than animals. But rather than eliminating animals entirely, there is a strong argument in favour of making meat production – the inevitable – better. It seems to me responsible to acquaint yourself with how meat and fish have been produced and to work out ways of balancing your food costs to offset the little extra you might spend on better quality meat and fish.

An aside on nostalgia for soya

The room is decompressing. Ecstasy has given way to what can only be described as a kind of tantric *savasana* and everyone is lying down: eyes closed, bodies clammy, downy hairs (among other things) erect.

---

* Michael Pollan, *The Omnivore's Dilemma: A Natural History of Four Meals.*

I lie looking at the ceiling, a tangle of rainbow bunting tacked to awnings that need paint. To my left there is a mantelpiece upon which Buddha sits resplendent between today's offering, a tin of Portuguese condensed milk, and an old photo of three scantily clad folk at the Rio Carnival. In the corner of my eye I can see my friend on a mattress, in a knot with *her* new friend, a carpenter. Their positions are much like those of the other couples strewn across the floor, panting, blinking, twitching.

I have just spent the last hour in a chakra-breathing workshop. That hour was like a microcosm for the whole weekend I've spent here in rural Dorset. (This is my thirtieth birthday present from the friend I am here with – less the 'yoga retreat' I was promised than a new age community with a penchant for tantra.) For 45 minutes, an electronic backing track escorted us through the gamut of our seven chakras but I'm sure almost everyone stopped at the second (sexual) chakra. We were supposed to have our eyes shut throughout but, intrigued to know who was making each of the rhythmic grunts and hums and cries, I peeked, frigidly bouncing in my solitary back jack. One woman is moving so vigorously in hers – her pubic bone clutched in one hand, the other reaching for the sky – that she might catapult across the room.

Now, however, with the audio switched off, I can only hear the whisper of pheromones and the odd plate clatter from the kitchen next door. While the others bask in sensual epiphany, nether regions aflutter, the cilia in my nostrils quiver. I can smell lunch. A scent wafts through the bay window, a curiously comforting scent given my extreme discomfort.

There is nuttiness to it. It smells whole and brown. There is garlic (of course there's garlic, everyone here in their fleece jumpers trails a whiff of allium around with them), but also the sweet scent of beans and mashed root veg. When it comes to facing this feast, I am not wrong about any of the above. There are greens too, naturally, and plenty of natural yoghurt, and the kind of coarse home-made hummus that looks like wet cement. It is the sort of 'looks awful, tastes great' vegetarian cuisine with which I grew up. Soya beans galore! The kind of veggie food that gives veggie food a bad name, but that I love unapologetically.

I ate a lot of soya when I was young. Being vegetarian narrowed your options considerably back then, and soya was one of the few high protein ingredients that at once offered sustenance and an effective vehicle for flavour when you cooked with it. Most commonly, Mum used it in dried form and I remember the packaging vividly, inexplicably transparent so that you could see the grisly grey pellets within. This went by the ever-glamorous name 'Textured Vegetable Protein' (TVP) – my, hasn't branding moved on – which, when soaked, took on a mince-like texture and appearance. She would routinely use it for lasagnes and pastas, flavoured with lots of soy sauce. (I still enjoy it, but I will spare you a soya section.)

But because I grew up eating it, and particularly because its source was usually Mum, I find soya to be one of the most nurturing things to eat now, its blandness a comfort, its cheapness and versatility a signpost of home. If there was one good thing to come out of my accidental tantric holiday, it was the coddling scent and taste of soya.

Deborah Madison

It's Friday afternoon and, just as I'm contemplating a Campari, Deborah Madison hits the morning coffee. Such is the time difference between London and Galisteo, the small town in New Mexico that she calls home. I've not met Madison before but there has been a warmth in our brief email exchange prior to speaking: little details of her life shared – references to her husband (the painter Patrick McFarlin), walking the dog, and to that cup of coffee she's just sat down with – so this already feels like more than a cold call. Plus I've loved her books for years: *The Greens Cookbook*; the seminal, and recently updated encyclopedia, *Vegetarian Cooking for Everyone*; *Vegetable Literacy*, which cultivates intuition with plant-based cooking in its readers; and the charmingly illustrated bible of solitary dining, *What We Eat When We Eat Alone*, which she co-authored with McFarlin.

Madison is the accidental doyenne of vegetarian cooking in America. Accidental because, she says, vegetarianism found her. In 1969, she went to live in San Francisco's Zen Centre to practise seated meditation. The group of fifty with whom she was living in the cooperative decided to be vegetarian early on – 'among us was a nurse who had been given a turkey by her hospital, and that started a conversation . . . there was a precept about taking life.' They needed a cook and Madison's hand shot up. Meat wasn't especially important to her, and its exclusion didn't feel like a sacrifice. What's more, cooking vegetarian food presented a challenge; it was like no food she had cooked before. She started to experiment with macrobiotics, 'which not everyone liked, so I soon gave that up. The point was practising Zen meditation, not food. But sharing meals *did* matter, and people needed to relate to the food.' So she began to combine some lesser-known Japanese ingredients – hijiki seaweed, miso – with mainstream ingredients like eggs and cheese.

In the seventies, vegetarian food was, says Madison, 'a drab, revolutionary thing, part of what was going on around Haight-Ashbury.' It was, in other words, the edible counter-culture. 'We were alarmed by processed foods. The first forays by young people into vegetarian food were pretty bleak: grains, grits, groats, and not a lot of skill.' It was at the Zen Centre, then, that Madison started to cook – with only meat-free produce – but it was also where her eyes were opened to growing produce of her own. Despite both her father and brother being botanists, she admits to having been unaware of how to grow food until she was in her mid thirties. She recalls planting sage in the impacted ground of the Zen Centre with a pickaxe and becoming 'hooked'.

I hear Madison sip her coffee down the phone. Listening to her speak, I long ago forgot about that Campari (one of my mantras while researching this book was not to romanticise things, but I find this particularly difficult when I imagine, wistfully, life in California in the 1970s). Back then, however, there weren't many places to find good heirloom vegetables, and the variety was poor; this seems extraordinary set against the Bay Area of today, where the possibilities are ostensibly endless if you're in the market for heirloom varieties of tomato and other seasonal produce. From the 'supermarket' of dreams, Berkeley Bowl, to the Ferry Building farmers' market, it's a locavore's utopia. In the seventies, the emergent Californian cuisine was based on fresh and local produce, including meat. But the particular emphasis on seasonality – on eating according to what the changing climate made available – in turn put focus on broadening the range of plants available to grow, cook and eat: 'Vegetables were just starting to get interesting and there was an appetite for new varieties. I'd bring seeds back from France to play with in the kitchen.'

By this point, Madison's playground was Greens, a non-profit vegetarian restaurant which, with the Zen Centre, she opened in 1979 in San Francisco's Marina district. Madison was a founding chef. 'It was possibly the first farm to table restaurant that actually had a farm,' Madison tells me. She'd put the new varieties she'd found in France to work in the restaurant – deep red lettuces, golden beets, rocket – and describes serving each table a hollowed-out pumpkin with soup made with its flesh, as well as cream, sage and Gruyère; the style was rustic, home-grown and anti-cliché, 'I was very strict about there being no sprouts, parsley and orange slices on plates.' Herbs like borage and lovage, sorrel, cucumbers, Sweet 100 tomatoes and pumpkins flourished, though Madison is quick to clarify that not everything they used in the kitchen came from the farm, 'the California coast is very foggy and it's impossible to grow nightshades – peppers, tomatoes, eggplant – so for those things we started to build a network of growers we knew.'

Greens spored Madison's career as a go-to authority on vegetarian eating, 'I got stuck with that label.' (What she doesn't reveal until later is that she'd already been labeled 'greens' – sort of. Her middle name – brilliantly – is Leafy. She's not sure whether that was her botanist father having fun or a misspelled tribute to the doctor who delivered her, one Dr Leary.) She admits to being more intuitive with vegetables than she is meat, more comfortable when writing about produce. And yet she struggles with the vegetarian label. It's limiting, it misses the point. 'I didn't want to stand on the veggie platform because I feel it is better to change the system than to turn your back on it.' I sense weariness in her voice. She is tired of being typecast as a vegetarian chef – 'that is not who I am' – and equally tired of trying to convince journalists that she is otherwise. Her interest lies more in biodiversity than in giving vegetarians protein-rich alternatives to meat, which is simply a by-product of specialising in plant-based cookery. 'This is my position,' she says, 'I don't buy meat. I'm often given it, because a lot of my neighbours are ranchers, and in those instances I take it, I say thank you, I cook it, I eat it. I feel like rejecting a person's food is like rejecting them.'

Eating everything, but being selective in doing so, enables people to have a more proactive role in remedying some of the problems that industrial food production has introduced. It also gives us first-hand involvement in helping the food chain operate like the joined-up, holistically integrated system it is designed to be. Madison promotes this more nuanced approach, 'it can be more complex to take the middle of the road argument' [rather than sequestering animal protein from your diet]. Despite the inadvertently vegan character to lots of her recipes, she says, 'vegans seem to have everyone's attention right now. The absoluteness of veganism is something that vegans wear like a badge of honour. But veganism isn't as clear and clean as they seem to think. You can till a field for corn but, well, birds might be nesting there. You're taking away their habitat. Have they thought about that? You know, life is really messy and difficult. Things die no matter what you do. You don't get a free pass just because you're a vegan.'

There are significant human implications to widespread conversion to veganism too: 'it turns our backs on the culture of making foods, like cheese, which families have spent generations making, curing . . . all of this *matters*. If people keep cutting out cheese, then there go hundreds of years of talent, art, skill . . . I find it abhorrent.' I don't think vegans are at risk of taking over the world – or not yet, anyway – but I take her point, a kickback to the blinkered omission of whole food groups without considering any of the broader implications. 'Just because things contain animal protein, they aren't necessarily a cruel act,' she says. She quotes a Tibetan monk she once met. He'd posited that it was more ethical to eat a yak than a chicken, because a yak feeds many. This does strike me as ethically sound, and all the fish- and sometimes chicken-eating 'vegetarians' suddenly seem all the more ludicrous.

As with all my subjects for this book, I had originally approached Madison by asking for an interview about the food she grew up with. When I steer the conversation this way, there is a pause, a tentative intake of breath. She confesses that she was worried about me asking these questions. She grew up with 'horrible' food. Her mother, Winifred, was an artist, not interested in cooking, and took money out of the food budget to make sure her children had music lessons. This seems at odds with the fact that Madison's father had had dairy farms in upstate New York, producing wonderful butter and cream, she says, with milk from Guernsey cows. Latterly, the family moved to California's San Joaquin Valley and lived surrounded by walnut orchards. Though it is possible that this pre-empted Madison's ardour for good produce, the superior ingredients that surrounded her family home didn't translate into exciting meals. 'Food in our house was fairly indifferent. We sat at the table every single night, for sure, but we just got through it.' When her mother came to eat at Greens for the first time, she couldn't be persuaded to eat more than a cup of soup and a green salad.

And yet, when I press Madison for her examples of food nostalgia, no matter how few and far between, she comes up with the goods. Every September, her father would make concord grape pie; the flesh and skins of grapes were milled, mixed with flour, corn starch and sugar and baked in pastry. 'Concord grapes came to America in 1853 and my family moved to California in 1953, exactly a hundred years later. I always like the synchronicity of those numbers.' Madison still makes the pie once a year. Then there's prune tart with almond custard, which she makes each Thanksgiving. Oh, and pumpkin pie, of course. 'I feel sad if there aren't these opportunities for these little food memories. They're touchstones for the past.' Though the three dishes above are all desserts, I guess it's because they were special occasion dishes that Madison retains such gilded memories of eating them. Her parents were otherwise vigilant about junk food 'which, in the fifties and sixties, was already everywhere. We'd have a root beer float, like, once a year. I wanted all that stuff – the coke, the chips, the candy – because I wanted normalcy, but I'm so grateful I was denied it now. I just don't have a taste for junk food.' That Madison is ambivalent about sugar recalls Bee Wilson's thesis in *First Bite* – that our eating habits are learned in early childhood.

She does have a taste for coffee though, and I for that Campari. Just as Madison's day is beginning in New Mexico, mine is coming to a close in London. We resolve to speak again – more about biodiversity, less about vegetarians – and bid goodbye. She has a labradoodle to walk, and I head downstairs to fix myself a drink.

Vegetables

In Madrid I lived above a mini-market called Eroski. It was one of those smaller incarnations of a big chain that had all the essentials you might need from your local store. In my case: wine, giant jars of lentils, and those amazing plain-salted potato chips that Spain has perfected – all small luxuries that would have been pricy back home in London. But better than all of the above, better even than a cheeky issue of *Hola!*, were the vegetables. Oh, the vegetables.

As Spanish vegetables go, I don't think Eroski sold particularly head-turning ones. I probably could've skipped down to the fancy new Mercado de San Juan in nearby Chueca and bought more impressive, possibly organic, corn, lettuce and broccoli from towering pyramids that made the mini-market's selection seem a bit poxy. But what made this array of vegetables in my local, completely unremarkable shop look so wonderful was the sheer *normality* of varieties that were not only 'other' to me, but – as far as I could see – entirely Spanish and predominantly seasonal. The white asparagus that grows in the dark, so cruelly stunted, I thought, until I cooked with it and marvelled at its tenderness; the giant, sweet, yellow onions crying out to be caramelised; and the raf winter tomatoes, my favourite discovery, rather ugly as tomatoes go, with deep

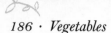

ridges and a deceptively green, thick skin. Many times I
wondered why the *abuelas* loaded up on them – they looked so
under-ripe, where was the redness that promised sweetness?
Over time, I realised that raf *were* fantastically sweet and ideal
for stuffing, or cutting up into wedges for vividly flavoured
platefuls embellished with nothing more than good olive oil,
perhaps a strand or two of anchovy, and a herb.

Good, native fresh produce was a given at that little Eroski
in Madrid, and the same is true of supermarkets across Europe.
In Sicily, I found gluts of navel oranges, lemons and kumquats,
long aubergines, artichokes and heavenly datterini tomatoes in
the local Carrefour. In France – in the Loire Valley, Burgundy
– I drove past fields of muddy onions seeping allium stench and
loaded boughs of apples, pears, and mirabelle plums, only to
find these most indigenous of goods picked and ready to buy in
the Monoprix supermarket down the road. I'm not saying we
should all shop in supermarkets, but the reality is that, a lot of
the time, many of us do. So how brilliant that there are places
where supermarkets champion local and seasonal produce,
and that these places don't charge over the odds, don't dress
them up as a luxury or make them the reserve of the farmers'
market classes. In my experience, European supermarkets
are places where good fresh food is available to all. (Though
people understandably, and rightly, wax lyrical about farmers'
markets – they champion small producers whose interests
lie in producing excellence over volume – I do feel that local,
seasonal produce should be more widely available and more
affordable.)

Cooking with vegetables a lot has definitely made me a
more discriminating shopper. I am lucky to live near a very
good fruit and vegetable shop, so avoid buying fresh produce

at the supermarket whenever possible. From one week to the next, I am able to witness produce as it waxes and wanes, the rising or falling quality of seasonal vegetables. How, as I type in February, the purple sprouting broccoli is starting to glow with sumptuous colour while the romanesco cauliflowers are shrinking; the sack of sweet potatoes overflows while the aubergines slump, wistful for the sun; a few months later – as I edit this manuscript at the end of May, the bulging Wye Valley asparagus – which came in so early this year – boasts its fine physique above a sackful of new Jersey Royals and bunches of radishes, peppery magenta globes that make me think of Peter Rabbit.

I think it is because of the seasons that many of my food memories involve vegetables. They punctuate the year in eating. How the sweet bite of a tender new potato boiled with mint and tossed in butter and salt announced the countdown to the summer holidays, when we would decamp to north Norfolk, a watershed in the year that lasted from the final spots of green turning golden on wheat husks to their harvest, after which I remember taking great pleasure in stamping down the crop stumps in my plimsolls. How a baked potato or a cauliflower cheese – workaday vegetables embroidered with cheese, pickle and ketchup – would herald going back to school, the descent into winter. The stretch of time when I was young – when nothing was expected of me, when everything was accounted for – was accented by the tide of foods with seasons, giving the year a narrative arc.

I try to cook with seasonal produce as much as possible, quite simply because the results taste better. It of course makes sense for vegetables to dictate what you eat; the very best examples of fresh produce will reveal themselves if you follow the seasonal calendar, revelling in greens of summer – asparagus, courgettes and peas – and roots of winter – Jerusalem artichokes, beetroots, turnips . . . There's no denying the Proustian palpitation I feel on biting into a sweet and crunchy June cucumber each year. All this said, I don't like to be evangelical about eating seasonally, which – as we've touched on – can still be an elitist game; I'd like this chapter to inspire you to follow the food calendar where possible but, more importantly, to let vegetables dictate your cooking – whatever that involves. It might come down to what looks nice in the shops on a given day, or it might be about taking the least showy, most mundane of produce and giving it a bit of chutzpah, a bold allure.

This chimes with what is becoming popular in restaurant land. Vegetables don't take the supporting roles they had when I was a child. Chefs like Ottolenghi have made them headliners, glamorous stars under the spotlight where the table is the stage. Aubergines are no longer relegated to the dangly earringed and open-toe sandaled. The prospect of vegetarians coming to supper induces fewer sighs of irritation than once it did. In recent years, I've been asked to write features for mainstream women's magazines about the unprecedented rise of, variously, the aubergine, the avocado, the cauliflower as the centrepieces around which other ingredients revolve. Vegetables are cool. And while I have never been cool, I *have* always tried to cook in this way – not necessarily consciously, but because spells of vegetarianism, living with the meat averse and being skint demanded it.

Cooking with vegetables should be an act of complementing, not disrupting or disguising, their flavours and textures. Below I have outlined the things I like to do to make vegetables – seasonal or otherwise – the best they can be. Following this is a set of recipes that use some of the most everyday vegetables, the staples I can always find, whether native or imported, and thus those which laid the foundations of my early vegetable experiences: beetroot, broccoli and cauliflower, carrots, sweet potato, onions, cabbage, carrots, green beans, pumpkin and aubergine.

1. *Salads*

A salad is an orchestra, a single entity of ingredient parts that harmonise together. What constitutes a salad harmony is more subjective than it is in music, a question of individual taste.

Yes, a salad is also a personal thing, a thrown-together jumble of raw and cooked, of fresh and store-cupboard, of acid, salt, fat, texture, sometimes sweetness. I eat salad all the time, 'salad' being a loose term referring to an ad hoc jumble of things-I-have-slash-things-I-fancy-eating. Sometimes that means being unorthodox and, if someone is watching, perhaps quietly buttressing myself against the knowledge that this is not how they would do things. Thus, like other personal things, eating salad is something which, often, I'll do in private.

As a kid, my culinary *pièce de résistance* was a bag of pasta boiled and dressed with vinaigrette, mayonnaise and ketchup, then spiked with various things from tins – olives, sweetcorn, tuna. I spent my GCSE study leave eating iceberg lettuce with tuna (again), feta and balsamic vinegar. The other night, yearning for watercress and dill when I spotted them in the greengrocer, I combined a bunch of each in a bowl with a raw, grated beetroot and some cinnamon, lemon and garlic dressing (see page 260). Salad is the place where my cravings congregate and wait to be answered. It is also a broad church

and everybody seems to have a different, often quite prescribed, approach to what a salad should be. For me, the most important thing in a salad is that every part of my mouth lights up as I eat it. A bowl of cold rice or barley can form the basis for a salad, as can leaves, as can anything that promises some vegetables and variety.

For a crowd pleasing salad, I'll often make a (more conservative, but no less delicious) Middle Eastern inspired chopped salad: gem lettuce, good tomatoes, cucumber, spring onion and a few different green herbs all chopped up into dice then dressed with olive oil, lemon and salt (add grilled flatbread and you have a fattoush, or remove the lettuce, swap the spring onion for red and introduce some olives and feta and you have a Greek salad).

2. *Boiling*

I grew up on boiled veg that veered on the side of too crunchy. And sometimes this is nice, particularly the stalks (clearly the best part of a broccoli – conveniently not everyone agrees). Far too crunchy veg can, however, feel like a punishment. I like broccoli, and let's use broccoli as the example here, that has been boiled enough that a knife glides through its stalk. I prefer boiling to steaming because that means you can let the salt in the water gently season the vegetable in question. This also means you need to add less (or no) salt at the end. The best way of serving boiled veg like broccoli is in these combinations:

a) with good extra virgin olive oil and a squeeze of lemon

b) with soy sauce and some grated ginger

c) lightly fry 1 minced garlic clove and a big pinch of chilli flakes in 2 tablespoons of extra virgin olive oil, then toss in the vegetables

d) parboil the veg, then finish them off in a tin of coconut milk, a squeeze of lime and pinch of salt

e) do what my colleague Dale Berning Sawa (my go-to authority on freestyling with Japanese ingredients) does and boil or steam a vegetable – best of all sweet potato, turnip, daikon, or squash – until tender before frying it in a tablespoon each of miso, soy sauce and honey. Fry for 5 minutes or so on each side over a medium–high heat for a beautifully caramelised, handsome topping for a bowl of rice or punchy cold addition to a bento box.

3. Roasting

To roast a tough vegetable – like roots and squashes – chop them up into chunks (I rarely bother peeling them). Preheat the oven to 200°C/400°F/Gas mark 6, tip the chunks into a roasting tin and glug over some extra virgin olive oil so that each morsel glistens. Season generously. I like to throw a lemon half or two in there, then a whole garlic bulb halved width-ways halfway through cooking. Roast in the oven until they are tender (if they start to burn but aren't cooked within, cover with foil and continue roasting for a while). Then, squeeze the roasted garlic and now slightly blackened lemon over the veg. Any of the yoghurt condiments on pages 230–235 make good accompaniments.

Alternatively, wait for a tray of roasted veg to cool, then dress it with an oil-based dressing. Or, integrate your leftover roasted veg into a salad. One of my favourite things to do is to eat roasted squash on top of peppery leaves like rocket, then to finely chop preserved lemon and scatter this on top, perhaps with a handful of seeds, before dressing the whole lot with good oil, lemon or vinegar and salt. If you have roasted garlic to add to this dressing then so much the better.

You can also convert leftover roasted veg into soups like the roasted squash and coconut soup on pages 200–201. Fry some finely chopped onions and a clove of garlic, then add these to any leftover roasted veg, cover with vegetable stock and, if you like, a tin of coconut milk. Let this cook at a rolling boil, until the vegetables are really soft, then blitz, season and add a squeeze of lemon if it needs a burst of acid. Serve with a swirl of olive oil and a dollop of yoghurt.

4. Charring

I am anti induction hobs for two reasons. First, because I like to be able to gauge the power of the heat I'm cooking on by eye. The other is that a flame is essential for charring vegetables like aubergine and onions. Charred vegetables provide the ideal opportunity to put a yoghurty sauce concoction to work for which, you may have now realised, I need little encouragement.

5. Braising

To braise is to fry and then lightly stew an ingredient, a form of twice-cooking. You can also boil and then sauté an ingredient which in Italian is called *ripassati*, or repassing. I learnt this from our *Guardian Cook* columnist, Rachel Roddy. It could be done with any vegetable you would just as happily eat boiled, because that's what you do first. Boil the vegetable in liberally salted water, then fry it, gently, in good extra virgin olive oil with a garlic clove. This is a wonderful technique to use for broccoli, romanesco cauliflower, fennel and courgette. I suppose currying is another form of braising: frying then simmering ingredients in combinations of spice, onion, garlic and a liquid in which to cook it all. For a simple curry, dry fry 1 teaspoon each of cumin, coriander and onion seeds in a pan over a low heat to release their aromas, then add oil, chopped onion, minced garlic and ginger, followed by 1 teaspoon of garam masala or curry powder, 1 teaspoon of ground turmeric, plenty of salt, and then fry whatever vegetable you want to curry in this spice mixture – stirring frequently – before adding a tablespoon of tomato paste, a tin of coconut milk and the juice of a lemon or lime. Bring to the boil, reduce to a simmer and let this bubble away until the vegetables are cooked through and tender. It tastes its best when left to cool and then reheated, and served with plain rice, yoghurt and chutney.

BEETROOT CURRY

Like Prince, this is a celebration of purple and makes you want to dance. Unlike Prince, it's incredibly straightforward – almost embarrassingly easy to make. Beetroot is brilliant at absorbing flavour and, when grated, cooks quickly. Get everything else ready fifteen minutes before you want to eat, then add the beet. I like to eat it alongside a dahl – two sorts of side dishes that combine to make a complete meal that is also good for you – then top it all off with a dollop of natural yoghurt.

———

SERVES 4–6

2 tbsp solid coconut oil

2 tsp mustard seeds

2 tsp cumin seeds

2 onions, finely chopped

3 garlic cloves, finely chopped

4cm piece of fresh root ginger, grated

½ tsp dried chilli flakes

2 large beetroots, roughly grated

½ tsp ground cardamom

1 tsp ground cumin

1 tsp garam masala

1 tsp ground turmeric

salt and pepper

———

1. Heat the coconut oil in a deep-sided frying pan or heavy-based saucepan over a low–medium heat, add the mustard and cumin seeds and fry for a couple of minutes. They will start to pop and become fragrant.

2. Add the onions, garlic, ginger and chilli to the spices and sweat over a medium heat for a further few minutes until soft.

3. Add the beetroots and the remaining spices, stirring to ensure the even distribution of flavour, then continue to cook over a medium heat for about 3 minutes, until the beetroot wilts and absorbs the flavours surrounding it. Season to taste and serve with rice and yoghurt, or as part of a spread of other curries.

BEETROOT, FETA, DILL

I often use feta, crumbling it over countless roasted vegetables. The natural sweetness of root veg like beetroot, parsnip and carrot is wonderful, but I find it quickly becomes monotonous. Feta is a good, fresh, salty foil to this – goat's cheese would work well too. Apart from dill, which I buy at the grocer, the ingredients in this recipe are all ones that I perennially have to hand. This showcases my love of herbs, their almost clashing aromatics married so beautifully by the sweetness of fresh beets and salty feta.

———

bunch of beetroot (4–5 medium beetroots)

2 tbsp extra virgin olive oil

1 tbsp red or white wine vinegar or sherry vinegar

handful of feta, crumbled

bunch of dill, chopped

salt and black pepper

———

1. Place the beetroots in a large, deep saucepan and cover with water. Bring to the boil, then reduce the heat to a simmer and cook until tender. Drain, leave to cool, then slide the skins off the roots.

2. Chop the beetroots up roughly, toss in the oil, vinegar and some seasoning, then sprinkle with the feta and dill.

ROMANESCO AND ANCHOVY BREADCRUMBS

You could equally make this with cauliflower or broccoli, but I need no excuse to cook with lurid, monster green romanesco cauliflower with its gorgeous turreted florets. Whether or not you dress it with oil before sprinkling on the breadcrumbs depends on the richness of the rest of your meal, I think, but the marriage of vegetable, oil and lemon juice is a beautiful thing. Just saying . . .

———

SERVES 2–4

1 romanesco cauliflower, broken into florets

juice of 1 lemon

drizzle of extra virgin olive oil (optional)

salt

For the anchovy breadcrumbs

2 tbsp extra virgin olive oil

½ tin anchovy fillets in oil (about 25g), and 1 tbsp of their oil

pinch of dried chilli flakes (I like pul biber)

grated zest of 1 unwaxed lemon

40g breadcrumbs

———

1. Bring a large pan of generously salted water to the boil. Drop the bigger cauliflower florets into the water, followed by the smaller ones a minute or 2 later. Cook until a floret stabbed with a knife slides effortlessly off the knife and back into the pan, then drain.

2. While the romanesco is cooking, make the anchovy breadcrumbs. Heat the oil (both olive oil and the oil from the anchovies) in a frying pan then add the chilli and anchovy fillets and fry for 1 minute. Add the lemon zest and the breadcrumbs and fry the mixture for a couple of minutes until crispy.

3. Drain the romanesco and toss it in the lemon juice, a drizzle of oil, if using, and half of the anchovy breadcrumbs. Arrange on a plate and scatter with the remaining breadcrumbs.

SWEET POTATOES WITH GINGER AND CHILLI

This is so simple, so good for you, and so full of flavour. It makes for many a weeknight meal at home with wilted spinach and braised lentils.

———

SERVES 2

2 sweet potatoes

2 tsp solid coconut oil

4cm piece of fresh root ginger, peeled and grated

½ chilli, deseeded and finely chopped

———

1. Preheat the oven to 200°C/400°F/Gas mark 6. Prick the sweet potatoes and transfer them to the oven to roast for about 45 minutes. They will start to ooze bubbling sugar where you have pricked them and will turn soft when they are done.

2. Cut each potato open and spoon on a teaspoon of coconut oil, a pinch of grated ginger and some finely chopped chilli.

REVOLUTIONARY WHOLE ROASTED CAULIFLOWER

When my friend Rosie Birkett made this, it converted my boyfriend from cauliflower cynic to cauliflower disciple and, in a home in which meat is cooked relatively little, this has had a revolutionising effect on weeknight suppers. Cut into 'steaks' and served with a good condiment – the seasoned yoghurt on page 230 or the tarragon and avocado dip on pages 279–280 – this makes quite the centrepiece around which potatoes or rice and carrots can dance. A high achieving dish indeed. Mark Twain once said that 'cauliflower is nothing but cabbage with a college education.' I'd add that this cauliflower has a first class honours degree.

———

1 large cauliflower

extra virgin olive oil

sea salt

———

1. Preheat the oven to 200°C/400°F/Gas mark 6. Remove all the leaves from the cauliflower and scoop out a chunk of the main stalk, about half the size of a ping-pong ball. This will mean that the very tough, dense stalk cooks at the same rate as the rest of the vegetable.

2. Drizzle the cauliflower with oil, making sure it is completely coated, then put it on a roasting tray with a generous pinch of salt.

3. Place in the oven and cook for 1–1½ hours. It should be going golden brown on the top when it's ready and ideally you want a cauliflower

that still has a little toughness about its stalks so that the steaks remain intact when you slice into it. Serve cut into 'steaks'.

4. A variation on the above is to cut the cauliflower into thick steaks while it is still raw, then lightly steam these, so that they are only partially cooked. Then, drizzle with a little olive oil and whack 'em on the barbecue.

ROASTED SQUASH AND COCONUT SOUP

Squash can be monotonous and cloyingly sweet. I don't dislike it, but often feel it's missing something. The citrus and ginger with which it is roasted here gives it a bit of zing, layering flavours onto the vegetable – with which the coconut milk joins in – to give it acidity, richness and complexity. Serve with a swirl of the seasoned yoghurt on page 230.

———

SERVES 4–6

1 butternut squash, peeled, seeded and diced

4 tbsp extra virgin olive oil

2 generous pinches of sea salt

2 tbsp solid coconut oil

4cm piece of fresh root ginger, finely chopped

grated zest and juice of 1 lime

1 tsp honey

1 onion, finely chopped

1 x 400g tin of coconut milk

500ml vegetable stock

black pepper

yoghurt, to serve

———

1. Preheat the oven to 200°C/400°F/Gas mark 6. Lay the squash out on a roasting tray, drizzle with 3 tablespoons of the olive oil, sprinkle with the salt and toss to coat, until the squash is glistening with oil. Transfer to the oven and roast for 25 minutes.

2. Remove the tray from the oven, add the coconut oil, chopped ginger, lime zest and juice and honey to the roasting tray, toss and return to the oven for a further 10–15 minutes, until the squash is tender.

3. While the squash is roasting, heat the remaining oil in a frying pan, add the onion and fry until it is soft and beginning to take on some colour, then transfer to a large saucepan with the coconut milk and vegetable stock.

4. Remove the squash from the oven and put all the contents of the roasting tray in the saucepan. Bring to the boil over a medium heat, then remove and blitz with a hand blender until smooth. Serve with plenty of black pepper and a dollop of yoghurt.

CAPONATA

I find this classically Sicilian sweet and sour stew makes (thanks to the aubergine, I suspect) a veggie centrepiece more effortlessly than other meat-free dishes. My version is fairly orthodox, with the exception of the optional inclusion of harissa, which I discovered thanks to a happy accident when I didn't have any tomato paste. It adds a pleasing piquancy and, though not authentic, isn't too much of a push given North Africa's proximity to Sicily . . . I go big on flavour – for a milder caponata, use just one tablespoon each of vinegar and sugar.

SERVES 4–6

6 tbsp extra virgin olive oil

2–3 aubergines, cut into chunky dice

2 onions, roughly chopped

2 celery sticks, roughly chopped

1 tsp dried oregano

1 tbsp tomato purée

1 tbsp harissa (optional)

1–2 handfuls of pitted olives

2 tbsp capers

2 tbsp red or white wine vinegar

2 tbsp sugar

salt and black pepper

1. Heat 2 tablespoons of the olive oil in a large frying pan, then add the aubergines and a pinch of salt and fry until golden and starting to crispen on the outside. You may need to top up the oil by a tablespoon or 2. When you're satisfied with how they're looking, remove them from the heat and set aside.

2. Heat the remaining oil in a heavy-based saucepan over a low–medium heat, add the onions, celery and oregano and fry for about 10 minutes: you want them soft, translucent and glistening in oil.

3. Add the remaining ingredients, mix well, then reduce the heat to low and cook, covered, for 30–40 minutes, stirring intermittently, until you have a soft, fragrant stew. If it starts to look a bit dry, add a small splash of water (not too much – you don't want to create a loose sauce).

CHARRED AUBERGINE, SMOKED GARLIC AND WALNUT DIP

The combination of sweet, sour, charred aubergine and garlic makes for a mouth disco. You will need a gas cooker or some kind of open flame.

—

SERVES 4

2 aubergines

100g walnuts

1 smoked garlic clove

2 tbsp extra virgin olive oil, plus extra for drizzling

2 tsp pomegranate molasses

squeeze of lemon juice

big pinch of salt

big handful of dill

fresh pomegranate seeds, to serve (optional)

———

1. Pierce the top of each aubergine with a fork or other pronged instrument. Hold them over an open flame and leave them lying over the flame for about 10 minutes, turning them occasionally. You will start to smell their skins charring. You might hear them letting off steam, bursting the skins as they cook. This is good! Once they are soft and charred all over, remove them from the flame and transfer them to a board, cut off their tops, then cut them in half lengthways.

2. Break the walnuts into small pieces and toast them lightly in a dry frying pan. Keep an eye on them and move them around often as they burn quickly.

3. As soon as the aubergines are cool enough to handle, peel the black skins from the flesh and discard. Try to get as few of the little chips of black skin into the flesh as possible. Tip the flesh into a sieve placed over the sink and let the excess liquid drain off for 5–10 minutes.

4. Tip the strained flesh into a blender with the smoked garlic clove, the olive oil, pomegranate molasses, lemon juice and a big pinch of salt and whizz until smooth. Transfer the mixture to a bowl and fold in the toasted walnuts and the dill, holding back a little of each for garnishing. Drizzle some more extra virgin olive oil over the top, the last of the walnuts, the pomegranate seeds, if using, and dill, and serve with toast.

GREEN BEANS BRAISED IN TOMATOES AND WINE

For beans – and many vegetables, for that matter – to come together with a sauce like this, I find you have to cook them beyond what feels comfortable. There's a time and a place for them being tender, but in this instance, you want green beans that flop like rabbit ears within a crimson, winey stew. Delicious as a warm side dish, it's even better cold the next day with good bread, and perhaps some salad and cheese.

―――

SERVES 4

4 tbsp extra virgin olive oil

1 onion, sliced into half moons

2–3 garlic cloves, finely chopped

1 x 400g tin of good-quality plum tomatoes

300g fine beans or French beans,
topped and tailed then cut in half

1 glass of dry white wine

½ tsp red or white wine vinegar

juice of ½ lemon, plus extra to serve

½ tsp ground cinnamon

handful of dill, chopped

salt

―――

1. Heat the oil in a sauté pan over a low heat. Add the onion, garlic and a little salt and sweat for about 10 minutes, until golden.

2. Add the tomatoes, break them up in the pan with the back of a spoon or a knife, and mix well. Cook for a further 5 minutes.

3. Add the beans, stir to coat them in the tomato mixture, then add the wine, vinegar, lemon juice and cinnamon and bring to the boil. Reduce the heat to a very gentle simmer, cover, and cook for 45 minutes–1 hour until the beans are soft, sweet and at one with the tomatoey, winey, juicy goodness. Season with salt and lemon juice to taste, stir in the chopped dill, and serve.

GREEN BEANS WITH CURRY LEAVES

The heady scent of curry leaves is infectious, not least because it promises their flavour. I like using them in simple preparations so that they can really sing. You want them to thoroughly infuse the oil and coat the beans here, accented by the heat of the chilli, a spike of lime and whiff of garlic.

—

SERVES 2–4

400g green beans, topped, tailed and cut into 3

1 heaped tbsp solid coconut oil

2 garlic cloves, finely chopped

10 curry leaves

½ tsp dried chilli flakes

150g peanuts, toasted then bashed (optional)

juice of 1 lime

handful of coriander, torn

salt

———

1. Blanch the green beans in generously salted water for 4–5 minutes or until they are tender, then drain and refresh under cold running water. Set aside.

2. Melt the coconut oil in a frying pan over a medium heat, then add the garlic, curry leaves, chilli flakes and the beans and cook for 3–4 minutes, until the beans start to blister a little. Transfer the beans to a serving dish.

3. If you are planning to use peanuts, toast them in a dry frying pan now, then bash them up so that you have a kind of coarse meal.

4. Toss the beans in the lime juice, torn coriander, salt and, if using, peanuts, and serve.

GREEN BEANS WITH MISO

I sometimes get a veg bag from a farm called Nama Yasai in Lewes. It's run by a husband and wife duo – he's British and she's Japanese – and the resulting haul includes Japanese ingredients suited to the southern British growing calendar: musically named things like kabu, daikon, mizuna, and shiso leaves as well as burdock root, Japanese squashes, nasturtium and garlic chives . . . I have taken my Nama Yasai bag as an opportunity to play with other Japanese flavours, without any claim or even attempt at authenticity, only a fond appreciation for the way in which Japanese flavours can lift ordinary

vegetables into something else entirely. I made these green beans in miso with my leftover garlic chives and shiso leaves – both entirely optional ingredients below – but now make it regularly because: a) I always have miso and soy sauce lingering around, and b) who doesn't love green beans?

———

big handful of green beans (about 300g), topped and tailed

1 tbsp butter

1 garlic clove, chopped

1 tbsp red or white miso paste

1 tbsp soy sauce

juice of ½ lemon

salt

garlic chives, chopped and/or shiso leaves, to garnish (optional)

———

1. Cook the green beans in a large saucepan of generously salted water for 4–5 minutes, or until tender and no longer crunchy. Drain and set to one side.

2. Melt the butter in a frying pan over a low–medium heat and add the garlic, sweating it for about 1 minute before adding the miso, soy sauce and lemon juice. Swirl the ingredients around. The miso may need a little coaxing to liquefy – if you need to encourage it, add a teaspoon of boiling water.

3. Increase the heat and tip in the beans. Heat them through, then transfer to a serving dish and sprinkle over the chopped garlic chives and/or shiso leaves to serve, if using.

BRAISED RED CABBAGE WITH APPLE

If you're perennially surrounded by vibrant, flavourful fresh produce – as they are in the Mediterranean – then preparing food can be a question of intuitive assembly – letting good, simple flavours congregate on a plate – rather than actual, well, cooking. In Britain, however, our expectation is that vegetables will need a boost. While I pine for more variety than potatoes and cabbage in winter, ultimately I'm grateful for the limitations that climate has imposed on northern European cuisine, making us resourceful with the store cupboard when the fields give little. Without them, I'm not sure this classic sweet and sour dish would exist. It was one of two things my maternal grandmother could cook; the other was roast pheasant. The two would often appear on the table side-by-side when my mum was growing up. She cooked less and less as she became older, especially when she and my grandfather divorced in the eighties. My food memories of her mainly involve biscuits and ready-made canapés from M&S, so it is fondly that I imagine her in cooking mode, bringing together the bird and this sweet and sour braise for her brood. You'll need at least 3 tbsp each of vinegar and sugar – I like to go for it, but only you know your own tastes.

SERVES 6–8

olive oil, for frying

1 onion, finely chopped

glass of red wine

1 apple, unpeeled and cut into small cubes
1 medium red cabbage, finely shredded
equal parts red wine vinegar and brown sugar, to taste
200ml vegetable stock
salt and black pepper

————

1. Heat a glug of oil in a heavy-based saucepan, add the onion and sauté until translucent.

2. Add half the red wine to the pan along with half the apple, half the shredded cabbage, half the red wine vinegar and half the brown sugar, and stir thoroughly. Repeat with the remaining wine, apple, cabbage and vinegar.

3. Cover with the stock, bring to a simmer and cook for 30 minutes, stirring occasionally, until the cabbage is cooked through, limp and gloriously purple. Season to taste.

4. You may feel you want more acidity or more sweetness. If so, add more red wine vinegar or sugar to suit your tastes.

CARROTS WITH SMOKY BACON

This is another one I grew up with, and it transports me right back to my grandmother's Sunday lunch table. It's a pretty relaxed affair, so don't take the recipe below too seriously and do play around with quantities. It's even better if made in advance, giving the flavours time to mingle. To borrow the words of my aunt Mary on the matter, 'Doesn't really matter if you end up over-cooking it as it still tastes fockin' delicious!'

———

SERVES 4–6

knob of butter

olive oil, for frying

1 yellow or white onion, finely chopped

a few rashers of smoked bacon, finely chopped

6 carrots, cut into 0.5cm discs

salt and black pepper

———

1. Melt the butter with a glug of oil in a frying pan, then add the onion and bacon and fry until soft and starting to turn caramel in colour.

2. Add the carrots, a small pinch of salt and a dash of water, stir, and cover. Cook for a few minutes, until the carrots are tender. Serve sprinkled with black pepper or, even better, leave to rest a while before serving.

Obsessions

—— · ——

. . . every session I had no fewer than sixteen girls with 'allergies' . . . They had cleverly developed 'allergies', I believe, to the foods they had seen their own mothers fearing and loathing as diet fads passed through their homes.

Gabrielle Hamilton, *Blood, Bones & Butter*

Every body is made with the intimate imprint of the familial body story.

Susie Orbach, *Bodies*

One way or another, I have spent most of my life obsessing over food. I wake up thinking about it, and by the time I'm dressed and ready for work, my day in meals has been mapped out. That's partly a pleasure thing – I really love eating and all the rituals that come with it: buying food, cooking it and, yes, tasting it as I go along; understanding where food comes from – the country, the region, the restaurant, the chef, the field in which it grew; and, as this book will testify, all the stories that cultures, families and individuals attach to certain foodstuffs.

I also live in horror of feeling hungry, of not having access to food when my body demands it. Knowing where my next meal will come from acts as a kind of mental security blanket. My mum suggests this fear goes back to a time in my sleepless infancy when she, desperate and sleep-deprived herself, took me to see a healer. The healer tested a lock of my hair, declared I mustn't have dairy, wheat or most fruit and, overnight, cut them all from my diet (until that point, they had been virtually *the only* things in my diet). To borrow Mum's words, I starved. For a few months she tried to get me to like soya milk, rice cakes and mashed avocado. When the sleeping continued to be problematic, probably because I was so hungry, she gave up and I resumed a normal diet.

This anecdote was something of a revelation to me, and goes some way to explain a childhood of overeating for fear of not having food when I needed it. I find it really quite amazing that the habits I've developed around eating – neurotically filling up my stomach for fear of it becoming empty before another opportunity arises – might date back to a time that I can't remember. I still really struggle with feeling hungry – or 'hangry', in my case, such is my inability to control my emotions when I need food.

I also have problems understanding the people who 'forgot to eat lunch today'. Sorry? *How* did you forget to eat lunch today? Did your stomach not rumble? Did you not see or smell someone else's lunch and think, maybe, you'd quite like some too? Did you not feel weak mid-afternoon and think a cup of tea and a biscuit could sort you out? So many questions enter my head, questions with answers I will never understand.

I can be very tongue in cheek about this, call myself 'professionally greedy' or quote Julia Child saying, 'People who love to eat are always the best people' (which I stand by). It's true that my work justifies dedicating a disproportionate number of thoughts to food. I can also feel happy that I'm largely uncomplicated about attending to the needs of my stomach, that I don't have a problem with eating at meal times, and that I don't have, nor have I ever had, a serious eating disorder. My obsession with food is a healthy one. Or is it?

I'm not so sure. Arguably, no obsession is healthy because, by definition, 'obsession' implies unbalanced or skewed thoughts. In the last two years, I have had countless pitches from young women who have collectively become known as 'healthy' or 'clean eating' bloggers. I very rarely take the bait. This isn't because I don't think it's great that these young women are cooking and spreading enthusiasm for doing so among other girls. And this isn't because healthy food doesn't have a place in the supplement – quite the opposite. I am just unconvinced about how 'healthy' they really are. I am more concerned that the fever around 'clean eating' marks a shift in young women's obsessions with food; it makes hang-ups acceptable, authenticates the sequestering of entire food groups (wheat, gluten, dairy, meat, sugar, carbs, to eat only raw things, to 'detox', the list goes on) and, often, the self-diagnosis of 'intolerance' – all to justify an agonised relationship with food. Even the 'clean eating' moniker is flawed, suggesting that any deviation from a diet of kale, avocado and quinoa, is in fact 'dirty'. The very idea of 'clean eating' seems to send mixed messages while making the rapidly growing 'health' sector of the food industry a lot of money.

When we met, Susie Orbach made the solution to the problem of overeating seem so simple – 'eat when you're hungry and stop when you're full' – and when she said this I realised that it was a rule I'd never adhered to. For most of my childhood I avoided feeling hungry and would pig out at meal times. I had no problem with being seen to eat a lot because

I was a tomboy – but now that I think about it, being a tomboy became convenient and perhaps validated my overeating. I believe received wisdom dictates that if boys eat a lot, they do so 'heartily', they are encouraged, celebrated for their healthy appetites and growing bodies; but if girls have seconds, thirds, they eat 'greedily'. It is as though our bodies are not supposed to grow. In my case, perhaps my solution was to 'play boy' so I could eat what I wanted. Predictably, I became chubby. In the playground, I passed my size off as a badge of honour, saw my solid frame to imply strength and vitality. And I was happy with that . . . until I was a teenager, when feminine delicacy became the order of the day.

Suddenly, I became mortified by people seeing me eat. Embarrassed by my size, I felt that if others watched me eating they would make the link between what I ate and how I looked. So I started to eat privately, stuffing my face in the morning, then going whole days without eating, only to hurry home and devour a whole Soreen malt loaf in minutes. I would think about food constantly, either about how hungry I was, or about how disgusting I felt after overeating. My relationship with food, then, became a polarised one and I was, without realising, a typical teenage girl, as Orbach would have it; in *Bodies* she writes, 'Such concepts as appetite and satiety elude [teenage girls].' These obsessions around food – the causal link between eating and the body – do seem particular to girls, picked up from mothers and other role models.

TV programmes like *Man v. Food* indulge the idea that men should eat massive portions of meat, fat, bone, salt – and go easy on greens, 'cos they're girly, aren't they? – and provide the perfect example to juxtapose with how we are conditioned to think women should eat. There's no doubt about it, girls and boys are treated differently, both around the family table and by the food industry at large.

When I asked my mum about any differences she noticed between how my brother and I ate as kids, she quickly observed, 'He became obsessive about things.' I was intrigued. I thought girls were the obsessive ones? She went on to explain that, like many little boys, my brother had been a fussy eater but had got really into certain foods and drinks over the course of his childhood. Because he was fussy, his food enthusiasms were fed. He carried a beaker of juice like a rosary. He loved chicken nuggets, miniature vanilla cakes, chocolate yoghurts – and these were always in stock. Blimey, I think, it didn't pay for me to be so easy-going about what was put on the table . . . He had friends with similar foibles; one who would only eat peanut butter sandwiches, another who wouldn't eat other people's food so used to come to play with a 'packed supper' (I remember taking this very much to heart – who was this little bastard rejecting my mum's food?!). My partner, Freddie, whose food tastes nowadays I can't fault (bar his antipathy for cucumber), admitted to living on a diet of Domino's pizza for a year, which his mum brought to an end when she saw her credit card bill. Aged thirteen, he'd had sixty pizzas in three months.

I have wondered if my foibles would have been pandered to in this way. I do suspect that (perhaps unconsciously) boys' parents might give special dispensation at the table, their appetites encouraged, their preference for even the least nourishing of foods given a green light. In any case, they grow up celebrating food, their fixations with certain things – like Freddie and his pizzas – gratified; they're allowed to have 'phases'. For girls, however, being seen to be 'greedy', having what's perceived to be too much, having a taste for anything deemed too masculine, and so on, creates an environment of guilt and rebellion around eating. I wonder whether women's obsessions with food are more often than not born from denial while men's come from one of indulgence?

Food is a conduit to growth, to making yourself bigger and, by proxy, being more present in the world. By this measure, the way men are encouraged to eat demonstrates support for their taking up more space, while women – sustaining pressure to eat lighter quantities almost from the moment they are weaned – are presented with a conflict: growing versus shrinking in the most universal sense.

Susie Orbach

Susie Orbach doesn't cut the panettone as I would. She cuts across it, as though it were a loaf of bread. Had I not given her the panettone – had I kept it to eat at home, probably on a writing day – I would have cut into it like a cake, then spent the rest of the day plunging my fist in the cavity I'd created, mindlessly pulling out handfuls of doughy peel and spiced raisins, and shovelling them into my mouth. Susie's approach, it strikes me, would be a better way of knowing how much I'd eaten. Maybe I should take a leaf out of her book in future . . .

Anyone who knows anything about Orbach and her work, however, will know that measuring how much you eat is absolutely not the point. Across all her books, a unifying theme – mantra, even – is the essential, causal link between appetite and satiety. 'Food is good,' she says to me, returning to the table with her slice of panettone now toasted, 'but it only does you good if you eat when you're hungry and stop when you're full'. So it doesn't matter how she or I cut the panettone, nor is it helpful for me to think in terms of how the size of my portion might regulate my eating of it. Whether I have a carefully-measured slice or stuff handfuls of the fluffy dough into my mouth, what's important is knowing when I've had enough: to recognise my hunger for the panettone, to feed it, then acknowledge when I'm full. *That* is quite literally taking a leaf out of Susie Orbach's book. It all sounds so simple. And it is. Except it isn't. If only it were.

I visit Orbach at her home and practice in Hampstead, north-west London. We're a stone's throw from Freud's house, where he spent his final years, still home to The Chaise Longue; there is probably the highest concentration of therapists here of anywhere in London. Orbach has worked here for eight years and has lived in the area for most of her life. She is a practising psychotherapist, currently working on her thirteenth book, and was famously Princess Diana's therapist, instrumental in her decision to speak publicly about her eating disorders. Orbach's has been a career dedicated to addressing an escalating problem – anguished eating, fear of food – with particular emphasis on its implications for women. That said, it is not exclusively 'a women's problem'; she says the ratio of women to men who come to her practice is about 65/35: 'Most of the people I see have some kind of eating issue but think they just have to live with it. But very few come because of food – it just emerges that they have a distressed relationship with their body over the course of therapy.'

Many of Orbach's theories at first seem peculiar. *Fat is a Feminist Issue* (1978), for example, posits that despite a conscious longing to lose weight and be thin, women who eat compulsively have an unconscious desire to inhabit a larger body, to secure their place in a man's world. Reading about this for the first time, I felt intellectually stimulated but – and I say this as a woman with a lifelong tendency to overeat – I didn't necessarily identify with it. In *Bodies* (2010), she argues that the extreme emphasis on skinniness in the 21st century 'is both an outcome of the riches the West has taken for itself and some need to exhibit, among all this abundance, its opposite'. Again, I thought, I'm not thinking about the abundance of the West when I eschew fish and chips for a salad or go for a run – I just want to be thinner.

But, and this is crucial, if we were fully conscious of what motivated our desires then it would be easy to control them. It would be a piece of cake, if you'll excuse the pun, to resist shoving your hand repeatedly into the cavity of a panettone only to realise you'd eaten all but the crust while reading Orbach's *Bodies* while waiting at an airport (yes, this happened; yes, I am ashamed). The salad and the run are the flipside of the metaphorical panettone binge – a taking of appetite's reins, a 'fuck you' to hunger, an avoidance of guilt, and an undermining of the body's physicality. In a world where we are judged first on how we appear, our body shape outwardly signals our degree of self-control: fat is failure and thin is success. It all starts to make sense.

Orbach was born in 1946, the daughter of Jewish parents. Her father was a Labour MP and her American mother a teacher. She is pleased by the Lina Stores bag in which the now-sliced panettone arrived – Soho's old Italian deli was one of her mother's favourites, she says, adding that she spent 'proper money' on food. She remembers her using big flavours, like loads of garlic and onions, which were then less popular amongst the British. The kitchen was always full of exotic fresh produce like artichokes, but she also remembers her mother's excitement at the introduction of frozen foods, peas especially. With chicken, her preference was for *eyerlekh*, when the bird is cooked with its unhatched eggs still inside it; these young yolks made for a gorgeous chicken soup broth, 'that's the only dish the Jews know how to make that's way up

there . . . a high class consommé', she adds. For lunch boxes, she'd make Susie and her brother over-stuffed New York-style sandwiches, things like salami and lettuce on rye, which they'd promptly dump en route to school. Susie wanted to conform, to eat what the other kids at school were eating (and watched her own children do the same when she became a mother, refusing the vine leaves and falafel she proffered in favour of Marks and Spencer's chicken skewers). Children seem to override what their bodies might want in favour of what's socially required, which suggests there is something of a schism between our mind and 'body consciousness'.

The Orbach household never had bread, potatoes or rice, which was consistent with the popular nutritional theories of the time. These served as rules to rebel against. Her mother would swing between bi-annual stints on the Mayo Clinic Diet* (subsisting on eggs and grapefruit) and raiding a secret chocolate cupboard in the middle of the night. There was, says Susie, 'madness around food'. Today such madness is normalised. Her mother was obsessed both with eating and with not eating, the latter punishing the former. I ask her if she ever questioned this. She looks me straight in the eye, 'I grew up in a leftist family that said God didn't exist. That raises a lot of problems when you go to a nice C of E school. I grew up contesting. It was my modus operandi.' And this she has continued to do. Along with Luise Eichenbaum (co-founder of the Women's Therapy Centre), Orbach set up Endangered Bodies in 2010, a charity that

---

* A diet pioneered by the eponymous Mayo Clinic in the US, grounded in eating mainly fruit and vegetables, but which uses a pyramid system allowing lesser quantities of other food groups – carbs, sugars, fats, proteins. The diet set out to change 'bad habits' (like eating in front of the television) for 'good' ones (exercise), but is by some treated as a crash course, promising followers that they can lose 10lb in two weeks.

raises awareness of and campaigns to offset – undo, even – the body hatred so prevalent in Western culture. Our bodies are endangered because they are never enough for us, because we are taught to reject and change them from infancy. Orbach cites examples like parents using Photoshop on their baby pictures and the availability of apps such as 'Plastic Surgery Princess' on iTunes, which enables anyone aged four and above to import a photo of themselves and glimpse what they'd look like with, variously, rhinoplasty, liposuction and breast augmentation. The charity faces these various ongoing battles, but Endangered Bodies *has* succeeded in having the 'I feel fat' emoticon removed from Facebook.

Orbach is matter-of-fact about her early experience; she was dissuaded from eating starches and high-grade protein; her brother was 'probably' served first, could go out when he wanted and drive at the age of sixteen; as the daughter she was expected to eat more delicately, second, less. 'I never knew that sexism was operating until I was older,' she says. We are talking about something that was culturally very normal sixty years ago. She is more troubled by the fact that it's still normal now.* She sees a pervasive culture of fear-mongering among women, a domino effect of food and body hatred. This is a threat to future generations of women who, as girls, follow their mothers' tortured examples. Being on a diet is a natural state and food is an enemy to be afraid of. The message is fear when it should be excitement; restraint when it should be

---

* In *Bodies* Orbach talks about research by psychotherapist René Spitz: 'Studies showed that boys were breastfed for longer, that each feeding period was lengthier, that they were weaned later, potty-trained later, and even held more than girls; and this confirmed the emotional experience of the feminine psychology. It made sense. If, because of gender inequality, girls received less nurture from infancy onwards, their feelings of entitlement would be more limited and circumscribed.'

progress. 'The problem arises', says Orbach, 'when daughters are a projection of the mother's own failure to restrain, or a reflection of their mothering.' 'Daughters', she goes on, 'look like a calling card for their mothers. Children have become commodities.' This is one of the more chilling things she has said. I can remember feeling embarrassed by my failure to take after my own mother's thinness. I sometimes still am; I feel the world looking at us side by side and trying to work it out. In an effort to take things into my own hands, I've tried all sorts of things to emulate my mother's shape, convinced that with 50 per cent of her genes, I can have what she has if I put my mind to it. I was vegetarian for twelve years. I've tried cutting out wheat, dairy, sugar and alcohol, aspects of the paleo diet, cooking from 'clean eating' blogs . . . 'Underlying all those things is a fear of food', says Orbach. 'You're saying to yourself, "if I can sequester this stuff then I can be safe within these parameters."' Diets, then, repackage an unhealthy relationship with food and have made it not only socially acceptable, but a booming business for the food and beverage industry. I feel very stupid.

It's not just me. Everyone I know starts to look really gullible, and I wonder *how* this has happened. We're not really stupid, we just want to be healthy . . . don't we? But this, for Orbach, is just the problem. In *Bodies* she says that obesity – the 'obesity crisis' as the press have it – is presented as a health issue in which the psychological underpinnings of appetite and the desire for thinness are bypassed. Rather than measuring our body mass index (BMI), a frivolous gauge that labels us 'overweight' or otherwise, doctors should be asking about hunger: if we feel it, why we feel it, why we eat when we don't feel it. '"The obesity crisis",' Orbach tells me, 'is an attempt to medicalise the issue, rather than looking at why people are drawn to food in the first place.' As I see it, her campaign is to reunite our minds with our 'body consciousness', helping us to function as an integrated, satisfied, healthy whole, our psyches in tune with our stomachs.

Orbach makes no exception of herself. She tells me that food acts as a prompt to tell her 'Oi, you're not dealing with something,' and that she monitors her eating habits only insofar as they are a byproduct of her emotional wellbeing. She prides herself on having had over forty years without significant conflict around food. She's clearly a food enthusiast too, I think, glancing at her bookshelves, which include the River Cafe and Claudia Roden's books and David Thomson's *Thai Food*, reflecting her more recent interest in eastern flavours, some Middle Eastern influences and her 'default mode' of Italian cooking. She eats pasta almost daily, a woman after my own heart. 'I cook every day,' she says, 'it's a source of pleasure. I suppose there are people who wander in their garden to relax, whereas I'll sauté an onion, not necessarily knowing what I'll do with it.' And with that, she picks up the bread knife and cuts herself another slender slice of panettone.

Yoghurt

— ❧ —

Yoghurt didn't always cool me down. In fact, it riled me right up. Sitting up straight, clean-plate, knife and fork together, smiling sweetly, every time, I'd ask:

'What's for pudding?'

'Yoghurt and fruit.'

My zero to sixty acceleration on hearing those three words was quite something: sweet smile turned to scowl, neatly placed cutlery once or twice thrown across the room. I was going to call the NSPCC, I said, this was neglect. It said it all, I thought. Other people's parents took them to McDonald's while we went to the Streatham wholemeal shop. Other people's parents bought them Barbies while mine gave us strung wooden puppets. Other people's parents fed them ice-cream, fondant fancies, Angel Delight for pudding . . . and the best mine could come up with was natural yoghurt with a cut up pear? Tree-hugging drivel!

Nowadays, obviously, many of the choices that my parents made for me are ones I continue to make for myself. And I've revised my feelings about natural yoghurt too, which back then seemed so boring, bland and sour – not to mention yoghurt in its least charismatic form. Since those days, natural yoghurt has become a staple in my kitchen, a calming, tempering ingredient, not the faux-pudding that triggered my petulant threats to call child protection charities.

BREAKFAST OF A
LAZY YOGHURT CHAMPION

If, like me, you've always got yoghurt in the fridge and a piece of fruit hanging around, this makes for a healthy breakfast oriented around the store cupboard. You could add anything you like here – some nuts, dried fruit such as apricots or prunes, a dollop of fruit compote, really, anything. The ingredients list below is based on what I most often have around. Do try it with the tahini and turmeric though (on separate occasions). Serving it with ripe banana or some roasted rhubarb (see page 268) would be especially good.

SERVES 1

2 tbsp natural yoghurt

2 tbsp fine oatmeal

1 tbsp desiccated coconut

1 tsp runny honey

1 tsp tahini or ½ tsp ground turmeric (both optional)

ground cinnamon, to taste (optional)

fruit or compote, to serve

---

1. Spoon all the ingredients into a bowl for one and mix together, possibly with a drizzle more honey (or even a dusting of cinnamon on top, should you please). Eat with fruit or compote.

LABNEH

Moving on to lunch . . . From yoghurt comes home-made cream cheese, otherwise known as labneh in the Middle East. Making labneh is simply a question of draining the excess whey from yoghurt. Tip the yoghurt into a tea towel and squeeze the towel tight, right around it. Hang the bundle from a tap overnight, and in the morning you will be left with a substance that resembles Philadelphia, though more sour. The taste of your plain labneh will depend on the type of yoghurt you use, plain or Greek being the mildest and most familiar while sheep's and goat's have more of a tang.

Labneh is great on toast with something pickled on top of it – I've really been enjoying pickled za'atar recently, which is now being imported to the UK – or with a drizzle of honey and some thyme leaves. You could also flavour your labneh before serving. Simply mix in whatever taste you want to impart – you could try cinnamon or garlic or lemon zest – and let the process continue as normal. When the labneh has been around for a few days, which means it will have hardened up a bit in the fridge, you can roll it into little balls. Put these in a clean jar and cover them with olive oil, plus any aromatics you might fancy. Again, this is great to have in the fridge for a quick lunch, spread across a piece of toast.

Yoghurt cools heat – both the temperature kind and the spice kind. This makes it an excellent condiment – a blob on the side of a plate of curry, for example, or a swirl into a bowl of soup – freshening the dish. In this sense it has what I consider to be a unique quality over other dairy products: creaminess without richness, and a very distinct flavour profile that can offset rounder, fatty ingredients. It's also a good vehicle for

other flavours – for salt, olive oil, garlic, spice, citrus – it's a mainstay in my fridge, ready to have herbs, nuts, lemon zest and olive oil blitzed into it for one of my dips or sauces, no two of which are ever the same (though I'm sharing five base ideas with you below).

SEASONED YOGHURT

This is yoghurt dressed up for a night out. The oil, garlic, salt and pepper just give it a little lift, and enhance its savouriness. It is great with lots of vegetable dishes or smothered over an open baked potato. It's also a good foundation on which to experiment – you could add almost anything which is, in fact, how several of the offshoot condiments below were born. It is particularly good with some lemon zest and juice and a bunch of fresh herbs added – dill especially.

———

400g natural yoghurt

2 tbsp extra virgin olive oil

1 garlic clove, minced

salt and black pepper

———

1. Combine all the ingredients in a bowl and season with a pinch of salt and pepper.

TAHINI YOGHURT

Flung across roasted vegetables, or on the rosemary potatoes (see pages 159–160) with some chopped up tomatoes and torn parsley for a 'Middle Eastern patatas bravas' mash-up, this is very good. Or, try it shoved into a pitta bread with salad and grilled halloumi cheese. In a piece for Guardian Cook, *the London restaurant Ducksoup included a recipe for chargrilled quail served with curry-spiced tahini and burnt lime. It was knockout; the sweetness of mild curry powder and sesame held in delicate balance with the citrus and blackened bird. Try adding a teaspoon of mild curry powder, especially if you're planning to serve it with meat, and pimp it up even more with some olive oil in which you've fried a few curry leaves.*

SERVES 2–4

1 tbsp tahini

3 tbsp yoghurt

juice of ½ lemon

1 tbsp extra virgin olive oil

1 tsp mild curry powder (optional)

salt

---

1. Quite simply, mix all the ingredients together and season with a pinch of salt.

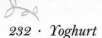

WHIPPED YOGHURT
AND FETA

Feta is a wonderful thing, but its saltiness can be intense. The yoghurt not only dilutes this, but gives it a looser, creamier (or 'whipped') texture for a condiment to roasted vegetables, or as a dip for raw veg and crisps.

———

SERVES 2–4

125g feta

4 tbsp yoghurt

extra virgin olive oil, to serve

———

1. Blitz the feta and yoghurt together in a processor or blender until smooth.

2. Transfer to a bowl and serve with a drizzle of oil on top.

SHADES OF
TZATZIKI

I have been forced to think outside the box with my tzatzikis because I live with a cucumber-phobe. As it turns out, this simple, Greek-inspired assembly of yoghurt, oil and garlic works well with other veg too. Witness this trio: carrot, beetroot and fennel. I like eating these alongside the winter spiced chicken (see pages 260–262) or just about any potatoes.

———

SERVES 4

2 carrots, grated, or 1 large beetroot, grated
or 1 fennel bulb, very finely chopped

1 tsp fennel seeds, toasted (if making the fennel tzatziki)

200g natural yoghurt

1 garlic clove, minced

2 tbsp extra virgin olive oil

salt and pepper

———

1. Combine all the ingredients and season to taste.

BABA GHANOUSH

In authentic Levantine circles, it would perhaps be considered 'unusual' to include baba ghanoush *in a chapter about yoghurt. Most recipes for this smoked aubergine and tahini dip-slash-salad don't include it. I originally added yoghurt to mine because I'd been over-zealous with the tahini and needed to temper the profusion of sesame. I've not done it differently since. In fact, I am convinced it makes it a better dish – one that goes further, the yoghurt offering a cooling white chariot to the burnt, nutty and grassy flavours of the aubergine, tahini and olive oil. You could go further here and drop in some chopped up baby plum tomatoes and lots of chopped parsley or mint. You will need a gas hob or some kind of open flame to char the aubergines.*

———

SERVES 4

3 large aubergines

1 tbsp tahini

1 tbsp natural yoghurt

juice of 1 lemon

1 garlic clove, crushed

2 tbsp extra virgin olive oil, plus extra for drizzling

pinch of za'atar, to serve

salt and black pepper

———

1. Pierce the top of each aubergine at the head with a fork or other pronged instrument. Hold them over as big an open flame as (safely) possible for about 10 minutes, turning them occasionally, until they are blackened, charred, flaky and soft.

2. As soon as they are cool enough to handle, peel the black skins from the flesh and discard. You will be left with a little bit of black skin, but try to keep it to a minimum. Transfer the flesh to a bowl and break it up with a knife and fork. (Don't put it in a blender. You want to keep the aubergines' texture and fleshy consistency.)

3. Transfer the flesh to a sieve placed over the sink and let the excess liquid drain off for 5–10 minutes.

4. Put the flesh into a bowl and mix in the tahini, yoghurt, lemon, garlic and extra virgin olive oil. Season with salt and pepper to taste.

5. Lastly, drizzle a little of your best extra virgin olive oil on top so that it makes little wells between lumps of aubergine. Sprinkle with za'atar and enjoy with good-quality fresh flatbread.

I think where it all went wrong between me and yoghurt when I was a kid was the instant association with pudding. It was a revelation to discover natural yoghurt used in so many savoury dishes, as is so common across the Middle East. Some years ago, I visited celebrated restaurant Çiya Sofrasi in Istanbul and ate a hot yoghurt and milk thistle soup. It blew me away. My yoghurt soup below is a riff on this idea. Pudding or otherwise, I doubt I'd have threatened my mum with the social services if she'd offered me this as a kid.

YOGHURT SOUP

This also takes inspiration from the yoghurt and barley soup – itself based on an Armenian recipe – in Yotam Ottolenghi and Sami Tamimi's Jerusalem. *Here, mine contains about half the amount of rice as the quantity of barley in their recipe, and relies on lots of seasoning, a swirl of good-quality extra virgin olive oil and whatever you decide to put on top. My favourite toppings include a handful of cooked and double-podded broad beans or a spoonful of saffron water (see page 111). You could also flavour the onions and garlic with any spice or herb you fancy while they are frying – Ottolenghi uses dried mint. Eat it as soon as it is ready, otherwise the rice will swell and the 'soup' will quickly become a savoury rice pudding.*

———

SERVES 4–6

100g basmati rice

50g salted butter

2 onions, finely chopped

2 garlic cloves, finely chopped

450g Greek yoghurt

2 eggs

juice of ½ lemon, plus extra to serve

extra virgin olive oil, to serve

2 spring onions, finely chopped, to serve

handful each of mint and parsley, chopped, to serve

salt and black pepper

———

1. Wash the rice several times under cold running water until the water runs completely clear, then place it in a large saucepan with plenty of salt (a good heaped teaspoon), cover with 1.5 litres of water and set over a medium heat. Bring to the boil, then reduce the heat and simmer until it is just-cooked, and still has a little bite to it. Drain, reserving the water, run it under cold water, and set both the drained rice and the cooking water aside.

2. Melt the butter in a frying pan over a low heat and add the onions. Cook over a low heat for 10 minutes, until the onion is beginning to soften in its buttery balm, then add the garlic and cook for a further 5 minutes.

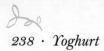

3. Add the drained rice to the butter, onion and garlic mixture, stir and remove from the heat.

4. Decant the yoghurt into a large heatproof bowl, beat in the eggs and season with salt and pepper.

5. Top up the reserved cooking water until you have 1.2 litres. Add the water to the seasoned yoghurt and egg mix, a ladleful at a time, beating continuously, until the yoghurt has warmed through. Doing this gradually will prevent it separating.

6. Transfer the yoghurt and eggs to a saucepan with all the water (you can use the same saucepan you cooked the rice in, if it's big enough), then add the rice mixture, lemon juice, and plenty more seasoning to taste. Place the pan over a medium heat just long enough for the soup to warm through.

7. Remove from the heat and serve in bowls with a swirl of extra virgin olive oil, a pinch each of spring onions and herbs, a little extra lemon juice and whatever other toppings you like.

Yoghurt also tenderises. In the recipe below, it combines with the mustard, garlic and spice to soften and season the meat over 48 hours of marinating. It also lends a cloud-like softness to the naan bread recipe that follows. The two are regularly eaten together in my home, complete with a lemony chopped salad, which ticks every box.

BAKED SMOKY YOGHURT CHICKEN

I like a quick-fix meal as much as the next person, but leaving the chicken to marinate overnight really pays off here. You want all the flavours to marry and mature, seeping into the pores of the meat.

SERVES 2–4

400g natural yoghurt

1 heaped tbsp Dijon mustard

1 heaped tsp pimentón

2 large garlic cloves, minced

2 tbsp extra virgin olive oil

big pinch of salt

8 boneless chicken thighs, skin on

2 onions, peeled and quartered

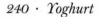

1. Mix the yoghurt, mustard, pimentón, garlic, olive oil and salt together in a large bowl. Put the chicken thighs in the bowl and coat them in the mixture, making sure each thigh is covered with the pinkish sauce. Transfer to a big, sealable freezer bag or cover the bowl with cling film and leave in the fridge to marinate overnight, or 2 nights if you have time.

2. When you are ready to cook, preheat the oven to 200°C/400°F/ Gas mark 6. Arrange the chicken in a baking tray and add the onion quarters, tossing them in the residual marinade that forms a moat around the chicken thighs. Bake for 30–40 minutes, until the tops and edges of the chicken are crispening up and developing a tan (the onion will be blackening in some areas – I consider this a good thing). At this point, should you want your chicken crispier or even charred, you can heat a frying pan and fry it for a couple of minutes.

3. Once ready, slice the chicken at an angle and arrange it on a board. Serve with a chopped salad and something to soak up the fatty, yoghurty juices, like plain white rice, or the naan bread on pages 241–242.

YOGHURT
NAAN BREAD

For pillowy and ever so slightly sour dough, yoghurt comes up trumps. If you don't eat all of these in one go with curry, or indeed with the recipe on the previous page, reheat the next day and fill with good fried or grilled bacon and some sweet chilli jam for a breakfast sandwich of dreams.

———

MAKES 6 NAAN BREADS

½ sachet of dried yeast (3.5g)

1 tsp honey

125ml warm water

250g strong white bread flour, plus extra for dusting

generous pinch of salt, plus extra for sprinkling

50g salted butter, melted, plus extra for brushing

4 tbsp natural yoghurt

1 tbsp ground cumin

black onion seeds, to serve

———

1. Mix the yeast, honey and warm water together in a bowl. The mixture should start to come alive and bubble after a few minutes.

2. Combine the flour and salt in a large bowl, then make a well in the middle. Add the melted butter, the yeast mixture, natural yoghurt and ground cumin and mix again, gradually bringing in the flour from the outside inwards to form a dough. Once the dough starts

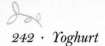

to come together, pick it up with your hands. You want a dough that is soft and yielding, not tough, so play it by ear and add more warm water if you need to.

3. Once the dough has come together, transfer it to a floured surface and knead for 5–10 minutes, until it is springy and smooth. Put it into a bowl dusted with flour, cover the bowl with a damp tea towel, and leave it at room temperature or in a warm place for 1–2 hours until it has doubled in size.

4. Divide the risen dough into 6 equal-size pieces then roll each portion into an oval shape just over 1cm thick.

5. Place a frying pan over the highest heat possible, then fry the breads 1 at a time, for about 3 minutes on each side. When you turn the naan over, brush with melted butter and sprinkle with a pinch of salt and black onion seeds. Once cooked, keep them warm in a low oven while the rest of the meal comes together.

6. Eat the breads with coconut dahl (see pages 103–105), egg, onion and coconut curry (see pages 43–45) or cashew nut, broad bean and spinach curry (see pages 262–264), a mountain of plain rice, and – naturally – a big blob of natural yoghurt.

I have also revised my approach to yoghurt as a pudding-worthy item. I was wrong. In the following recipe, I have married yoghurt and fruit – those three words that made my younger self kick off – in a trusted sweet thing to which I return, time and again.

YOGHURT, OLIVE OIL AND LIME CAKE

You could try throwing fruit into this – raspberries in summer, perhaps – or it is good as it is, with some roasted or poached fruit and crème fraiche, or just plain – moistly dense but strangely light – with a cup of tea. This cake was inspired by Claire Thomson's yoghurt cake, published in Guardian Cook *in 2015. I've swapped butter for olive oil, but both work well.*

———

SERVES 8

180ml olive oil, plus extra for greasing

100g pine nuts

2 eggs, lightly beaten

180g caster sugar

180g natural yoghurt

180g self-raising flour

1 tsp baking powder

grated zest and juice of 1 lime

———

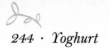

1. Preheat the oven to 180°C/350°F/Gas mark 4 and grease a 25cm springform cake tin with olive oil. Sprinkle a quarter of the pine nuts into the tin – the bottom of the cake will be the top when you serve it, prettily decorated with the kernels, so make sure they are evenly distributed.

2. Beat the eggs, sugar and yoghurt together in a bowl, then beat in the oil.

3. Add the flour, baking powder, lime zest and juice, and the remaining pine nuts.

4. Transfer the mixture to the greased cake tin and bake in the oven for around 45 minutes, or until a sharp knife or prong inserted into the middle of the cake comes out clean. Remove from the oven, allow to cool in the tin, then cover with a plate and tip over, removing the tin. Delicious with stewed fruit like pears, apples or plums.

Together

——·——

Eating is so intimate. It's very sensual. When you invite someone to sit at your table and you want to cook for them, you're inviting a person into your life.

Maya Angelou

Eat food. Not too much. Mostly plants.
Michael Pollan, *In Defense of Food: An Eater's Manifesto*

'This is what it's all about', says my uncle Justin, every Christmas as we sit down – finally – to eat. In fact, these days, it's rarely Justin who says it, so famous has the parody become. It's usually everyone else, in unison, while all 6'6" of Justin, arms crossed, nods at the head of the table saying, 'It's true.'

I don't think I realised quite how true Justin's truism was until Freddie and I decided to shun family and spend Christmas alone together in Sicily. Off we went, feeling very independent, with a mental list of things to cook for our first Christmas as a twosome – chicken, not turkey; roast potatoes with olive oil, not goose fat; local mustard greens (called *sanapo* in Italian) rather than Brussels sprouts. It was empowering . . . until the heating in our apartment didn't work, and the shower ran ice cold, and the power supply tripped, and the hob turned out to

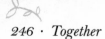

be a convection one, and – worst of all – we were faced with the prospect of roasting a chicken in what we thought was a snazzy new oven . . . but which was actually a microwave. The upshot of all this was that our Christmas cooking was limited to the stovetop. And while I'm always happy to eat pasta with tomato sauce overlooking a beautiful Mediterranean town, this wasn't particularly my vision for Christmas lunch. (We can laugh now. Freddie gave up on the chicken pot roast when his attempts at cutting its still intact neck off – not something Sicilian butchers often do for you, we discovered – proved unsuccessful. We took the chicken to the cheesemonger the next day and swapped it for a large chunk of pecorino. All's well that ends well.)

Anyway, suffice to say that spending Christmas eating pasta alone felt kind of sad. We might have been empowered, but the crux of Christmas – everything that all the endless menu planning and peeling and sprout prep and naff music and last minute trips to the supermarket for booze before the shops close on Christmas Eve, everything that all of that works towards – didn't happen for us. We missed what it was all about: eating with other people.

In celebration and in mourning, with those we hold dear and those we've just met, food sits at the centre of so much time we spend with other people. This is peculiar given how downright unattractive eating can be (I'm pretty sure my father can't have taken Mum for pasta or sushi during their courtship. If I'd had to sit opposite her wielding a fork and spoon with a plate of saucy spaghetti, not to mention the nightmare that is Mum with *chopsticks*, I don't think I'd have married her). But congregate around food we do. Regardless of the different directions life takes us, our varying successes and possibly failures, sharing in a meal is both a unifying moment and a leveller.

For my parents, and much of their generation, it would go without saying that when they were children the family would sit around the table together every evening. The table punctuated the day, forming the tenets of daily life, a rhythm. With the advent of women working in full time jobs came ready meals, TV dinners, and a grab-and-go eating culture that has transformed food from a sacred ritual – breaking bread – to mere fuel.

And yet, in conjunction with the demotion of the family meal from daily practice to special occasion, a deification of those who cook in the media has occurred. We love to watch people cook on television, indeed cookery TV shows are now primetime viewing. Chefs are often celebrities. It seems more than a little ironic that while we luxuriate in the sight of Nigella preparing her bundt cakes from scratch, we're so often shovelling down the easiest thing, something that was virtually ready to eat on purchase and bought in the spirit of expediency. The idea of 'convenience' has trumped the long game of shopping for raw ingredients, readying them and transforming them into nourishing meals. A fascination with watching people cook doesn't necessarily convert to wanting to cook more ourselves, in fact the opposite seems to be happening. Is cooking becoming a fantasy?

All this places more emphasis on the big occasions. Much as we chuckle at my towering uncle's sentimentality every Christmas, he's got it right. Modern life puts even greater importance on opportunities to eat and cook communally, because those opportunities now feel fewer and farther between.

Jamie Oliver

It's just another day in the life of Jamie Oliver.

The restaurant is a circus of tinkling keyboards, bright lights and reflective screens, broken English, jingling crockery and brushes exploding from make-up bags strewn across the bar. The main area is cordoned off by a Hungarian film crew here to record Jamie talking about his latest restaurant venture in Budapest; they give off that very particular film crew vibe of looking and sounding frantically busy, despite everything happening at a snail's pace. Jamie sits at the nucleus of this bustle, a spotlight illuminating his face, which is intermittently mattified by a giant brush. He patiently sips water as action is paused for the nth time.

I'm in the bar area with his team and a growing queue of journalists. *Vice* have just arrived, all tousled long hair and distressed leather. While we wait for our interview slots, we're shown into the basement, where we are each encouraged to find a nook in which to chat with Jamie. Each publication forms a little station at a table, ready for what will essentially be a speed date with the man himself. *The Andrew Marr Show* is setting up in the middle of the floor and, in the open kitchen alongside, a group of young chefs – the most recent intake here at Fifteen, Oliver's restaurant-cum-social enterprise, which offers young

people from a range of backgrounds ('some have been to prison, some have been homeless, many are underprivileged', Oliver tells me) into a kitchen apprenticeship – prepare staff breakfast. Giant plates of bacon and sausage emerge and send us journalists' nostrils aflutter.

Only a handful of people in the food world command such a high level of fame. Indeed, I've often thought the culture of the celebrity chef is a curious one, the extraordinary nature of celebrity so seemingly at odds with the ordinariness of food. It strikes me that this must particularly be the case for Jamie Oliver, such is the tension between his superstar fame and average Joe image; 'I feel like a really weird version of myself', he says, 'I've been totally shaped by the public.' Yet Oliver is insistent on his normality: he grew up in Essex, in a pub, in an environment where the attitude to food 'wasn't ninja sharp or single-minded.' Being relatable has been integral to his success, from the cheeky chappie on *The Naked Chef* who transformed cooking's appeal from 'for girls' to the thing 'that got you the girls' in the late nineties, to becoming a campaigner on childhood nutrition today. The seeming lack of privilege from which he has come makes him the ideal mouthpiece for some important messages about how to educate parents and children about diet. Oliver has a better chance than most of being heard.

Finally, his interview with the Hungarians is up and Jamie is shown down to my little nook. Our interview offers a brief lull in his day; with the cameras off, his exhaustion shows through. He knows I'm here to talk about kids and the importance of upbringing on our lifelong relationship with food. It's his hot topic at the moment, and yet he is visibly deflated, not the tirelessly enthusiastic Jamie Oliver on the telly. He says he is struggling to work out what his place is: 'I'm not a doctor, I'm not a politician, I'm not a CEO. So what the fuck is my role? I'm the voice of the public, I suppose, but they really struggle to engage on this one. We lack drama.'

It is as though I'm getting all the out-takes from his campaign spiel; he's fed up of sugar coating his words, no pun intended. The reality of how thousands if not millions of children grow up eating in Britain today is not palatable, so he might as well spit it out and bear the grim reality for all to see. 'We love thinking we're a democracy and that it's all cute and that we have personal choice. We can whine about nanny states . . . but fuck off. Even if we put in place what we need to, we'd still have huge freedom.' So what is it that needs to be put in place?

Oliver wants labeling clarity on all products available for public sale and, where possible, reformulation, 'The responsibility deal hasn't worked. Now it's about accountability, which means corporations are moving faster because they *have* to.' He wants the guarantee of nourishing school meals available to all children ('Eleven years ago, when I started campaigning about childhood nutrition, there were robust codes of practice for selling dog food, but none for children between five and eighteen'). He says that if the government ensures a good breakfast and lunch for children at school, half their nutrition for the year is accounted for, regardless of what they're getting at home, 'that should be worst case scenario, but historically too many are getting shit at school *and* shit at home. If we can at least be confident of what they're having at school, that changes the trajectory.' He wants legal standards for lunch boxes: 'Teachers are removing cans of Red Bull from seven year olds' lunch boxes, but there's no law to support that.' And, most famously, he campaigned for a national sugar tax, to attach financial penalty to the 'poison' that is refined sugar. The focus of this campaign was 'free sugars', the insidious molecules of glucose and fructose present in fizzy drinks, 'Big bottles of soda have no place in the home. Yet it's so normalised. I hate that I sound like a middle class freak when I'm the most normal bloke there is – I grew up around Coca-Cola and Britvic, for God's sake, I bottled them up!'

Oliver faces resistance from those who don't want to be told how to eat. But he insists that people don't have to relinquish their favourite treats in order to heed his advice. Much loved favourites – toast with lashings of marmalade, apple crumble, a bar of chocolate – are not the problem, he says, because 'we already know they're an indulgence'. He is not petitioning for joylessness, for the complete removal of sugar, but he does want to establish some ground rules ('because every game needs rules') to protect children from 'the surround sound din of life in which they are violated by junk food.' Still, many wilfully miss the point. I can see why he finds it so maddening.

I ask Oliver if it's possible to engineer a child's taste buds, and have hardly finished asking the question when he interjects, 'Yes, course it is.' How? 'Normality, rhythm, consistency.' He explains that, in an ideal world, what comes into the home via a weekly shop is always roughly the same. 'If you only have a certain palette of stuff coming into the home, then that's the normal stuff. On that basis, parents should feel empowered to let them have a candyfloss at the fair. The treats don't matter, as long as you've got your base covered.' He goes on, 'Types of food and ingredients are like friends, you get used to them. Children need exposure to runner beans or a corn on the cob to be comfortable with eating them. If you've got someone who's familiar with the Golden Arches (McDonald's) and doesn't know the difference between a potato and a chip, you can track a list of problems: obesity, diabetes, tooth extraction. As parents, we are marketers now.'

Oliver has mastered the art of reframing the world to look very cynical; he often comes out with these sorts of pithy sound bites designed to prick up ears and turn heads. It works. He says there are two ways of looking at the cereal aisle in the supermarket: one is just cereal, the other is real estate. 'The food industry has brainwashed the British public into thinking that they only have thirty seconds for breakfast every day', and that, therefore, our only option is a fleeting bowl of Coco Pops, making our blood sugar rocket before we've even left the house. He is laying bare a world in which even the most mundane decisions – what to buy in the supermarket, what to feed your kids for tea – are political choices on which your children's futures could depend. 'Before any food enters the equation, we've got a lot wrong. First, in Britain we drink less water than anyone else in Europe. Second, breastfeeding. Forget restaurants! It literally all comes back to the boob, and we are some of the worst in the world. Now, that's due to a mixture of reasons, working mums juggling more than they once did, perhaps how a generation of women feel about their bodies, but I'll tell you this: it's cultural. Thirty minutes on a plane away and there are similarly busy women with a similar pool of genes and they're doing just fine. We have a problem.'

A PR comes over. Out of the corner of my eye I see Andrew Marr arrive, and his cameraman looks expectantly in Jamie's direction. We've hardly touched on Oliver's upbringing, on his own children, the palette of food that enters *their* home, but I'm left with the feeling that Oliver has triple underlined the purpose of my writing this book. The trajectory of life rests on how we are educated to eat in childhood, and his purpose

is to improve that. My time is up. Jamie keeps on talking. 'You know, I was never political. I was a normal guy who was crap at school and only good at cooking. I never thought I'd end up in this place, campaigning for such basic rights – the right of every child to good health. I certainly never thought it would be so difficult.' And with that, it's lights, camera, action once again.

Spices and herbs

Sometimes you have to push yourself. That was what I realised as a twenty-one year old, imprisoned by feelings for someone with whom it would never work. There had been a lot of drama, and I needed to make a change. But change was daunting. Isn't it strange how familiarity at once comforts and unsettles?

I applied to study abroad for a year, far away, in America. Even flirting with the idea felt like an achievement, filling in the form a feat. I'm not sure if I thought I'd ever actually go, but I made sure I kept my chances low, putting up obstacles at every stage. I applied to the most competitive university, campus, courses, and at each juncture the opportunity welcomed me with open arms.

And I'm so grateful it did. That year in northern California reminded me of life's richness. Away from London, the physical world to which my sadness belonged, everything felt new, fresh, bright again. The future stirred me like the promise of salt spooned into unseasoned soup.

While my life particularly needed a shake-up at that point, I think travel always has a unique way of switching us back on in this way. It makes us sit up and pay attention to life, alert and open to the possibility of discovery, of doing things differently, even if you think you're comfortable as you are.

There's a lot about that year away that makes me think about cooking. The emphasis on fresh, locally grown produce in California, for a start. How major figures in the Californian food world – Alice Waters, Deborah Madison, both interviewed in these pages – encourage you to grow your own food, even on a small scale. How my palate's vocabulary widened and I learned to identify foods from certain cuisines of which I knew little – Persian, Korean, Mexican. (This was a major theme in my first book, *The Edible Atlas*, which took a whistle-stop tour of how flavour mutates as it migrates across the globe, how something so ubiquitous as a green sauce can be so utterly different from one region to the next, like Italian *salsa verde* [with parsley, basil, capers, anchovy] which is so distinct from the Canarian *mojo verde* [coriander, cumin, garlic, lemon]).

Most of all, that year in California put an accent on life, just as adding distinctly flavoured ingredients can accent a dish – a sprig of rosemary, a dusting of nutmeg, a jolt of chilli. Cooking with injections of flavour can reinspire our cooking just like that year abroad reinspired me; and perhaps above all other ingredients, it is herbs and spices that offer such glimmers of brightness when things start to trundle. This is probably why I refuse to follow a recipe when I make a tomato sauce for pasta or *salsa verde* for potatoes. These are things I eat all the time, several times a week, and I can keep the experience of eating them fresh by the changing the flavours and their proportions every time. It's important to keep the experience of cooking fresh too, I think, and again, it is herbs and spices that, in my cooking, offer up opportunities for adventure. A regular routine of dishes needn't be a prison if you keep the flavours diverse. A kitchen odyssey awaits in the form of fragrant leaves and scented seeds.

GREEN SAUCE

There is only one rule to green sauce and that is that it is green. That greenness comes from parsley and can be boosted by other green herbs should you want them. As with my tomato sauce, I've given you some foundations on which you can build. Fergus Henderson is insistent on 'five wonderful things' for his basic green sauce – capers, anchovies, extra virgin olive oil, garlic and parsley. He goes big on the garlic (twelve cloves!) whereas Lori De Mori and Jason Lowe go for a more modest single clove in Beaneaters & Bread Soup. *I only like a suggestion of garlic and often make this for a vegetarian, hence the exclusion of anchovies below (they are a delicious addition, though, just don't add salt if you use them). You could add a chopped hard-boiled egg at the end, which adds body and texture. I am a fan of this too.*

———

1 big bunch of flat-leaf parsley, finely chopped
(or half finely chopped, and half roughly chopped)

½ bunch (or as much as you like) of basil and/or dill and/or mint,
finely chopped

½ garlic clove, minced

handful of capers, rinsed and roughly chopped

handful of cornichons, roughly chopped

6 tbsp extra virgin olive oil

1 tsp white wine vinegar

salt and black pepper

———

1. Simply mix all the ingredients together and season with salt and pepper. You want it to have a thickish dressing consistency. Leave to stand for 10 minutes or so before serving, allowing the flavours to get to know one another.

Spices

As a kid, I felt about spices the way I felt about cats. I sort of liked them, but nervously. I was exposed to them, but only briefly and occasionally. Both had shown me their elegant sides, and both had caused me momentary agony once or twice (I'm thinking specifically of a black and white tomcat called Buttons and some chillies in a Szechuan restaurant that I inexplicably mistook for cranberries – no, I don't know why either). Both were to be approached gingerly.

Moderation isn't my greatest quality. If I like a good thing – a wine, a cheese, a chocolate – then I go for it. But, with spice, moderation is something that has been worth learning. So, as with everything mentioned in this chapter, if not this book, my own use of spice continues to be learned through trial and error. Spices are a great project for the experimental cook and, once understood, become a secret weapon. Subtlety is key. I find that a touch of nutmeg, or of cardamom, or a little sweet paprika, is a way of both coddling and piquing my palate. A well-spiced dish has an amazing ability to nurture, but also shows the cook to be one who has learned by practising.

I once interviewed chef April Bloomfield for our 'Last Bites' column in *Guardian Cook*, in which chefs fantasise about what their final meal might be. She would want a pork loin with a tomato sauce. Typically, I was less interested in the pork than I was its condiment, which she described to me as inspiring 'a flicker of recognition, but not so obvious that you could necessarily say what it was.' I so know what she meant; when you're eating something and your teeth are chewing and your taste buds are tasting and it's as though fingers are clicking in your head, trying to get just what that taste is – you know it, but what is it? *That* is how I try to use spice, for flashes of flavour you can't quite put your finger on.

Cinnamon is the spice I now use most. Its sweet scent still evokes childish delights – Danish pastries, apple pie, Christmas – but to pigeonhole cinnamon (and also nutmeg, cardamom, cloves and star anise) in the 'sweet spice' box is to limit both the spice and yourself. While it is brilliantly complemented by sugar, it is a fragrant addition to more of my savoury cooking than sweet these days. April's tomato sauce for pork loin is a case in point here, as is my baked eggs recipe (see pages 34–36) where the tomato sauce base is infused with cinnamon. One of my favourite things to do is the simplest of salad dressings: good peppery olive oil, the juice of a lemon, a hint of garlic,* a big pinch of ground cinnamon, and salt. Shaken up, this is a winner over all manner of bowlfuls, from butter lettuce leaves to bright, ripe tomatoes, wilted spinach and cold grains – and it is always brightened by fresh herbs.

---

* I have a complicated relationship with raw garlic in salad dressings, which I detail more in my 'Negotiating tradition' chapter. This cinnamon dressing, however, is brilliant with the briefest suggestion of it. Either finely grate half a clove, or peel and whack a whole clove with the back of a wooden spoon and drop it into the dressing before shaking it up. You want a trace of aromatic allium to dance with the spice and lemon.

CINNAMON, LEMON AND GARLIC DRESSING

The anti-vinaigrette. (Because it has no vinegar.) Slop this over a simple green salad, or any salad really, including the tabbouleh on pages 285–286. This makes too much for one salad unless you're feeding a crowd, but nae bother – it will improve in the fridge, the flavours mingling over the ensuing days.

———

8 tbsp extra virgin olive oil

juice of 1 lemon

¾ tsp ground cinnamon

1 garlic clove, minced

salt

———

1. Place all the ingredients in a jam jar with a generous pinch of salt, seal with a lid, shake and you're good to go.

SWEET-SPICED CHICKEN WITH PINE NUTS

A recipe in Sam and Sam Clark's Moro East *inspired this. Though the recipe below is a departure from their roast chicken with sumac and pine nuts on the flavour front, I have borrowed the technique of roasting browned chicken on a bed of spiced onions, and topping this with the lovely chewy crunch of pine nuts. The spice mix uses the 'three Cs' of* sweet spice — cardamom, cinnamon and cloves — and I recommend eating this with the lentil and turmeric rice fry (see pages 106–107), tahini yoghurt (see page 231) and a simple green salad.

———

SERVES 2 (GENEROUSLY)

2 tbsp extra virgin olive oil

6 chicken thighs, bone in and skin on

1 tsp ground cardamom

1 tsp ground cinnamon

½ tsp ground cloves

4 onions, sliced into half moons

½ unwaxed lemon, cut into small pieces (rind and flesh)

100g pine nuts

salt and black pepper

———

1. Preheat the oven to 220°C/425°F/Gas mark 7.

2. Heat half the oil over a medium-high heat in a heavy-based ovenproof casserole. Season the chicken thighs well and brown them all over. Remove from the pan and put to one side.

3. Mix the spices together. Add the onions to the still hot dish, season, and sprinkle with three-quarters of the spice mixture. Fry for 1 minute until fragrant.

4. Add the lemon, mix, and place the browned chicken pieces on top of the spiced onion mixture, skin-side up. Cook over a medium heat for a couple of minutes to give the onions some colour, then drizzle with the remaining oil and sprinkle with the last quarter of the spice mixture. Place in the oven and set the timer for 20 minutes.

5. Halfway through cooking, add the pine nuts (if you add them at the beginning of cooking they will burn). Once the pine nuts are burnished gold, you're ready to serve. In their version, the Clarks recommend removing the chicken and adding a little water to the onions, then reducing this down to a thick, sweet-spiced sauce, which is good.

So, subtlety is important when spicing a dish, as is balance. A dish or a meal involving spice needs it to be offset, or at least tempered by, other forces. It is for this reason that when I eat Indian food, I invariably have a pot of natural yoghurt right there to cool any heat and sour any richness that the meal's other component parts – chilli, fatty meat, clarified butter, spice blends – might have introduced. Many a cook has written about balancing sweet with sour, crunch and smoothness, seasoning and layers of ingredients and flavour. The recipes that follow emphasise this equilibrium.

Spices make you powerful in the kitchen. It is the smatterings and gratings and dustings of spice that have made many a secret recipe, and it is finding your own way with these that you can become the arbiter of your own.

CASHEW NUT, BROAD BEAN AND SPINACH CURRY

This demonstrates how easy it is to make your own spice mixture if you're stocked up on some basic, ground varieties: cumin (king of the curry), gaudy orange turmeric, ginger in its mellower dried form, and of course cinnamon and chilli. I love the meatiness of broad beans but if you can't find them, peas work fine instead.

———

SERVES 4–6

2 tbsp oil (preferably coconut, but rapeseed is good and vegetable is fine)

1 heaped tsp ground cumin

1 heaped tsp ground cinnamon

1 heaped tsp ground turmeric

1 tsp ground ginger

½ tsp chilli powder

1 tsp salt

1 x 400g tin of chopped tomatoes

6 tbsp natural yoghurt

6 garlic cloves

150g cashew nuts

300g frozen broad beans (or peas)

juice of ½ lemon

200ml warm water

200g spinach leaves

———

1. Heat the oil in a heavy-based saucepan over a low heat, mix the spices and salt together and add them to the oil. Fry for up to 1 minute, stirring constantly.

2. Add the chopped tomatoes and yoghurt, increase the heat until the mixture starts to bubble, then turn it down again and let it simmer gently for 10 minutes.

3. Grate in the garlic and add the cashew nuts. Cook over a medium heat for a further 5 minutes.

4. Add the broad beans, lemon juice and water, increasing the heat once again to bring it to the boil. Let it cook at a lively simmer for about 10 minutes until the liquid reduces by about half its volume.

5. Two minutes before you're ready to serve, add the spinach leaves, let them wilt in the curry, and dish up with plenty of chutney on the side.

Here are some other favourite spices:

1. Caraway seeds

These seeds have a strong flavour, so need to meet their match with something of comparable bite: capers, preserved lemons, salty olives, good vinegar and stronger herbs. You could substitute fennel seeds for caraway in the crackers below, but they also work in sweet contexts too. I once catered a Great Gatsby-themed dinner with a pudding of giant caraway cakes (in homage to the narrator Nick Carraway). These we decorated with stars, stripes and art deco designs in blueberries and strawberries and, yes, more caraway. Caraway makes a handsome couple with sweet root vegetables, offsetting the sugar with its gentle spice. Toasted seeds tossed with roasted beet or carrot, a little olive oil, a small splash of vinegar, some salt and a handful of chopped mint works well year-round. I also love the recipe on the next page, a Christmas favourite, in which caraway teases the sweetness out of cabbage alongside butter and onion.

SAVOY CABBAGE
WITH CARAWAY SEEDS

—

SERVES 4–6 AS AN ACCOMPANIMENT

50g butter

1 white or yellow onion, finely chopped

2 tsp caraway seeds

1 Savoy cabbage, shredded

200ml water

salt and black pepper

—

1. Melt the butter in a heavy-based saucepan over a medium heat and add the onion and caraway seeds. Cook for 2–3 minutes, stirring, then add the cabbage and sweat it in the butter, onion and caraway mixture for a further 2–3 minutes before adding the water.

2. Cover for 5 minutes, then remove the lid and move the mixture around some more. You want the flavour of the seeds to be evenly distributed and for the cabbage to look wilted without having lost its crunch entirely. You may need a little more water depending on the size of the cabbage you use.

3. Season to taste and serve.

2. Fennel seeds

These fat, green little morsels have an aniseed quality. They come from the fennel herb plant, but their liquoricey flavour can be quite full on, so I never use many at once. I love to fry a few with onions and garlic for a pasta sauce, or throw them into the bottom of a roasting tray with a chicken, onions and lemon (to make for a gravy of dreams). Sometimes I make a sauce for roasted fish – sea bass or bream – by melting butter, some olive oil, a squeeze of half a lemon (then throw the half in) and a sprinkle of fennel seeds. Also for these quick crackers:

FENNEL SEED, SPELT AND LEMON CRACKERS

MAKES ABOUT 24 CRACKERS

150g spelt (or wholemeal) flour, plus extra for dusting

80g cold salted butter, cubed

2 tbsp fennel seeds

grated zest of 1–2 unwaxed lemons (you decide)

2 big pinches of salt

lots of ground black pepper

3–4 tsp cold water

---

1. Preheat the oven to 180°C/350°F/Gas mark 4 and line 1 large baking sheet or 2 smaller baking sheets with baking parchment.

2. Put all the ingredients in a bowl except for the water and work them together with your fingers and thumbs, as you would a crumble topping. Keep working until you have evenly sized crumbs, then put 2 teaspoons of cold water in and work into a dough. Gather the crumbs into the developing ball of dough and add more water, a little at a time, until it is a single mass.

3. Roll out the dough on a lightly floured surface until it is 2–3mm thick, then cut into 24 squares and place on the lined baking sheet. Bake for 15 minutes until golden, then remove from the oven and leave to cool.

3. Nutmeg

Prettily named, gorgeously perfumed. Sometimes I think a dusting of nutmeg makes every beige food a little greater in its beigeness: custard, rice pudding, mashed potato. (I spoke to chef Anna Hansen recently about how to use tonka beans, a lesser-known 'sweet spice' from her native New Zealand, and she suggested using them much as you would nutmeg. Tonka beans have an aroma a little like smoked vanilla, with a hint of liquorice. They are by nature both balanced and subtle and, I discovered recently, ab fab with rhubarb. The recipe below would work with nutmeg or tonka – the former gives a more traditional character perhaps suited to the forced rhubarb of the winter months, while the fresh, less familiar taste of the tonka bean could hail the fat stalks of rhubarb in summer.)

ROASTED RHUBARB WITH BAY AND NUTMEG (OR TONKA)

The syrup also makes a lovely cordial. Any sugar will do, but the darker you go, the richer the syrup.

———

SERVES 6

6 rhubarb stalks, washed, trimmed and cut into 3cm lengths

6cm piece of fresh root ginger, roughly chopped

200ml cold water

6 tbsp sugar

2 bay leaves

1 nutmeg or 1–2 tonka beans, to taste

———

1. Preheat the oven to 190°C/375°F/Gas mark 5. Throw the rhubarb into a roasting tray, scatter with the chopped ginger, then add the water. Cover the tray with foil and transfer to the oven to cook for 20–30 minutes, removing the tray from the oven half way through cooking, lifting the foil and gently stirring the rhubarb (be careful to keep it intact).

2. Remove from the oven and sprinkle the sugar evenly over the fruit. Carefully mix in.

3. Drain off the liquid into a saucepan, add the bay leaves and grate in nutmeg or tonka to taste. Bring to the boil and simmer until you have a thick syrup.

4. Serve the rhubarb (hot or cold) with crème fraiche or ice cream and the syrup drizzled over.

4. *Pimentón*

This Spanish paprika comes in various guises – there's a sliding scale of sweetness and hotness – all of which are a pillar of Spanish cuisine, responsible for the signature smoky taste in chorizo and meaty stews known as *cocidos*. I love to throw a small pinch into bean stews, or over roast potatoes, sometimes fish, and have seen it inspire many a happy squint in those eating it. The best-known brand is La Chinata, but it remains fairly niche, which – in my case – has the happy effect of making the cook look more competent than they are. Buy yourself a tin of pimentón and start experimenting with it by dusting a little onto your food like a condiment or seasoning – tap it into sauces, marinades like the one for the yoghurt-marinated chicken on pages 239–240 and the plainer version of my baked eggs on pages 34–36. My friend Oliver Rowe introduced me to a kind of dry *brava* sauce seasoning of pimentón, finely chopped rosemary needles and sea salt. Toss your roast potatoes in this and never look back.

5. *Chilli*

I've never particularly geeked out on chilli. I like to use it simply, much as I use seasoning: to boost. I keep just three sorts: dried chilli powder, some very spicy dried chilli flakes, and *pul biber*, the crimson Turkish specks that give only a very subtle heat but have a unique sweetness. This really comes to life in the recipe below.

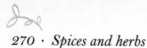

BAKED FETA WITH CHILLI, THYME AND LEMON

Piquant, salty and the perfect pairing to a glass of something delicious.

———

SERVES 2–4

200g slab of feta cheese

grated zest of 1 unwaxed lemon

generous pinch of dried chilli flakes (I like pul biber)

1 garlic clove, grated

5 sprigs of thyme

extra virgin olive oil

———

1. Preheat the oven to 180°C/350°F/Gas mark 4. Take a rectangle of foil and place the slab of feta in its centre. Create walls out of the foil's sides so that anything you add to the feta doesn't go rogue.

2. Sprinkle the lemon zest, chilli and garlic over the cheese, along with the leaves from 3 of the thyme sprigs, and drizzle with oil. Put the other 2 sprigs in whole.

3. Seal the foil and bung the package on a baking tray. Transfer to the oven and bake for 10–15 minutes until soft, yielding and aromatic. Devour with good bread.

KEDGEREE

This invariably awaited us on arrival at my grandparents' house, the kitchen a steamy announcement of smoked haddock cooked in milk. That scent can bring tears to my eyes, even now! I'm afraid a plate of kedgeree is still incomplete without several rounds of ketchup blobbed on the side – essential for me, if not for you. And go hard on the butter if you feel like it. For years my mum couldn't work out why her kedgeree couldn't rival Granny's, but then quickly saw, on watching her plonk half the butter dish in the pan one time, how it was quite so good.

———

SERVES 2–4

4 eggs

400g smoked haddock fillets

bay leaf

whole milk, to cover

150g basmati rice

50g butter (preferably salted)

1 onion, finely chopped

2–4 garlic cloves (depending on size), finely chopped

4cm piece of fresh root ginger, peeled and grated

1 heaped tbsp mild curry powder

1 tsp black onion seeds (optional)

juice of 1 lemon

handful of coriander, finely chopped

salt

———

1. Put the eggs in a saucepan of cold water and place over a medium heat. Bring to the boil and simmer for 10 minutes. Drain and leave to cool in cold water.

2. Place the haddock fillets in a separate saucepan with the bay leaf and pour over enough milk to cover them. Bring to the boil, then reduce the heat to low, cover and leave to simmer for around 5 minutes, then remove from the heat and let the haddock cool a little in the milk.

3. Wash the rice several times under cold running water until the water runs completely clear, then place the rice in a pan, cover with water and set over a medium heat. Bring to the boil, reduce the heat to a simmer, and let it splutter on the hob until it is cooked through. Drain and set aside until you need it.

4. Melt the butter in a large frying pan over a low heat and add the onion, garlic and ginger. Cook for 5–10 minutes until soft and starting to caramelise, then add the curry powder and the onion seeds, if using. Cook for a couple of minutes, then add a few tablespoons of the haddock's milky cooking liquor, squeeze in the lemon juice and bring everything together: add the cooked rice, flake in the haddock and season with salt to taste. Make sure every grain of rice is coated in the buttery spice mixture.

5. Fork the chopped coriander through the kedgeree, plate up, then arrange the eggs – peeled and quartered – on top of each dish. Serve with yoghurt, or even better, ketchup.

ROASTED SHREDDED BRUSSELS SPROUTS WITH NUTMEG

There's no reason why you shouldn't eat this outside of the holiday season.

———

SERVES 4 AS A SIDE

extra virgin olive oil

1 white onion, finely chopped

1 garlic clove, minced

300g Brussels sprouts, shredded

grated zest of 1 orange, and ½ orange for squeezing (optional)

nutmeg, for grating

handful of hazelnuts, halved and toasted, to serve

salt and black pepper

———

1. Preheat the oven to 180°C/350°F/Gas mark 4. Heat a big glug of oil in a frying pan, add the onion and fry for about 3 minutes, then add the garlic. Continue cooking for another minute, stirring, then remove from the heat.

2. Tip all the shredded sprouts into a roasting tray and mix with a big glug of olive oil, the onion and garlic mix, the orange zest, a grating of nutmeg, and season with salt and pepper. Transfer to the oven and roast for 20 minutes, tossing the mixture every 5 minutes.

3. Serve with the toasted hazelnuts tossed in and a squeeze of orange juice, if you like.

Herbs

I think about my Top Five Herbs a lot. In fact, I often think about my Top Fives in food groups – fruit, vegetables, carbs, cheeses – but I perhaps think about herbs the most because it's such a close-run thing, and changes from one day to the next. The biggest decision is between mint and basil. They can be used in similar ways: to spike fruits – tomatoes being the obvious, but also strawberries, peaches, apricots – to infuse salads and dressings and pestos, to finish off a jug of Pimms or to crown an Eton mess. While basil says 'Italy', layered in parmigiana, taking centre stage in pesto, or lacing a pasta sauce, mint definitively says 'Britain'.

I think mint takes the prize by a nose. Literally by a nose actually, because the smell of mint – both freshly picked and boiling away in a pot of new potatoes – is the resounding food memory of my childhood, my Proustian madeleine. Mint was always about; Mum grew loads of it or, rather, couldn't control the glut that took over our tiny garden – using it in everything during the summer was the only solution. I now use it a lot myself, often to freshen the sometimes-cloying sweetness of root vegetables in winter.

Basil is also an old faithful. I'm devoted to those soft, lurid leaves, whole or torn, which form the base of pasta sauces, crown braised vegetable dishes and salads like panzanella, and are the *raison d'être* of pesto.

PESTO

Arguably, the world doesn't need another pesto recipe, but here comes mine. I would encourage you to treat this as the roughest of frameworks. Though purists would doubtless scold me, pesto is a term I use loosely. I chop and change the greenery (hard to beat classic basil, but it's also excellent with tarragon leaves, rocket, wild garlic and sorrel, all of which bring their own character), the nuts (toasted cashews are lovely and creamy and I also like sharper walnuts) and the cheese (pecorino is an obvious, funkier, stand-in for Parmesan but it is good with any salty hard cheese — I tried Manchego recently, which worked a treat). The moment at which wild garlic comes into season is a special moment for the pesto enthusiast. I make my wild garlic pesto with two bunches of the stuff, plus 50g of basil but no added garlic. With sorrel pesto, you'll need less lemon.

SERVES 2–4

50g (at least) basil leaves

100g pine nuts, toasted

grated juice and zest of ½ lemon

1 garlic clove, chopped

50g Parmesan, grated

3 tbsp extra virgin olive oil, plus extra to make the sauce (optional)

splash of water (ideally pasta or vegetable cooking water)

splash of white wine vinegar (optional)

salt and black pepper, to taste

----

1. Place the basil, pine nuts, lemon juice and zest, garlic, Parmesan and olive oil in a food processor and blitz, then season to taste.

2. Now add water for the desired consistency – you want it more saucy for pasta (and in this instance don't drain your pasta too thoroughly – see pasta tips on pages 68–69) and perhaps a bit thicker for a dip. You could also thin it out with more oil if you like its richness. Add a splash of vinegar or more lemon juice if you like things a little sharper. Anything goes really.

It should really be no surprise that perfumed basil sits comfortably alongside the stone fruits of its season, like peaches and cherries. I can think of no better example than my friend Rosie Birkett's cake-meets-pudding below.

ROSIE BIRKETT'S PEACH, CHERRY AND BASIL PUDDING PIE

This is a version of a recipe in Rosie Birkett's cookbook, A Lot On Her Plate; *the fruit collaborates with the milk and egg to create a custard effect at the cake's centre. Yes.*

———

SERVES 8–10

unsalted butter, for greasing

6 basil leaves

4 ripe flat or regular flat peaches, halved and stoned

300g cherries, halved and stoned

30g flaked almonds

100g plain flour

200g ground almonds

2 tsp baking powder

pinch of salt

4 eggs

100g golden caster sugar

100ml whole milk

1 tbsp extra virgin olive oil

1 tsp vanilla extract

———

1. Preheat the oven to 180°C/350°F/Gas mark 4. Thoroughly grease a 24cm loose-bottomed cake tin with butter and place the basil leaves on the bottom of the tin. Cover them with the peach halves and cherries cut-side down and scatter with the flaked almonds.

2. Combine the flour, ground almonds, baking powder and salt in a bowl. In another bowl, whisk the eggs with the caster sugar until pale and fluffy. Add the milk, olive oil and vanilla extract to the egg mixture and whisk again, then fold in the flour and almond mixture, keeping as much air in the mix as possible.

3. Pour the mixture on top of the fruit in the cake tin, let it settle for a minute, then bake in the oven for 35–40 minutes, until the batter is golden. Remove from the oven and run a palette knife around the edge to loosen the pudding. Leave to stand for a few minutes, then put a wire rack on top of the tin and turn it upside down, removing the tin to let it cool on the rack.

Tarragon has to come third in my Top Five Herbs, the darling of my avocado dip (see pages 279–280), of *salsa verde* with a little twist, and a winner with chicken. As soft herbs go, tarragon dries very well, its intensity faded but its flavour still distinct. I don't know a better tarragon chicken recipe than my aunt Mary's. I've embellished hers with fresh tarragon here – I love the tongue-numbing green feathers which decorate this otherwise beige dish – and I find that using sour cream can tone down the richness of the dish a little, which is no bad thing. Serve this with plain rice and broccoli with lemon juice.

TARRAGON CHICKEN

If you can't get hold of fresh tarragon, use one tablespoon of the dried stuff. You could just as easily use chicken thighs instead of breast here, so long as the bones are removed.

———

SERVES 6

30g butter

30g plain flour

430ml chicken stock

2 tbsp white wine vinegar

150ml sour cream

60g Cheddar cheese, grated

2 tsp dried tarragon

4 fresh tarragon stalks, leaves only

1 tsp Dijon mustard

olive or rapeseed oil, for frying

750g chicken breast or boneless thighs, diced

salt and black pepper

———

1. Melt the butter in a saucepan over a low–medium heat, then add the flour. Cook for about a minute, stirring to form a paste.

2. Add the chicken stock and vinegar and whisk over the heat for a couple of minutes until the mixture thickens.

3. Reduce the heat, add the sour cream, cheese, dried and fresh tarragon, and mustard, season with salt and pepper and simmer gently for a couple of minutes.

4. Meanwhile, heat a little oil in a frying pan and fry the chicken for about 10 minutes, until the meat is cooked through.

5. Add the chicken to the sauce and you're done.

TARRAGON AND AVOCADO DIP

This green bowlful is always popular, either as a dip or a condiment. It is a conversation between the soft ingredients (avocado and yoghurt) and three punch-packing flavours that you wouldn't necessarily expect to find together: tarragon, cinnamon and citrus. The below is an approximation – I never make it the same way twice but it always turns out well. I use a mini processor but this is just as easily made by hand with a fork to mash.

———

SERVES 2–4

1 ripe avocado

5 tarragon stalks, leaves only

1 large handful of nuts
(cashew nuts, almonds and pine nuts are all good)

2 tbsp natural yoghurt

grated zest and juice of ½ unwaxed lemon or lime

big glug of extra virgin olive oil, plus extra to serve

¼ tsp ground cinnamon, or to taste

salt and black pepper

———

1. Halve and stone the avocado. Set 1 half aside and scoop out the flesh from the other into a processor or bowl.

2. If you're not using a processor, be especially diligent about removing the tarragon stalks and finely chop the leaves. Coarsely crush the nuts using a pestle and mortar.

3. Combine the mashed avocado half, chopped tarragon, crushed nuts, yoghurt, citrus zest and juice, olive oil and cinnamon and blitz or mash until smooth, seasoning with salt and pepper. Taste and adjust the seasoning – salt, pepper, citrus, oil – to your taste.

4. Finely chop the other half of the avocado and mix it in. This will give your dip a bit of texture.

5. Put the dip into a small bowl with a swirl of good oil on top and serve.

Frilly dill comes in fourth. I love to comb it through beans, scatter it on top of boiled potatoes and vinaigrette, tear it across scrambled eggs, or add it to beetroot with a little yoghurt and olive oil. Dill pays a refreshing compliment to pickles and caraway seeds – witness pickled beetroot with toasted caraway, a blob of sour cream and torn dill – and as a threesome they point in the direction of Eastern Europe. As well as the seasoned yoghurt with dill on page 230, I like to make a preserved lemon and dill relish which, again, brightens up roasted root vegetables, and makes a sharp alternative to green sauce with meat, from chicken to sausages.

DILL, PRESERVED LEMON AND CARAWAY RELISH

The number this serves depends on how you use it. As a relish beside meat, you're looking at one or two teaspoons per person, but if it's a dressing for vegetables, it should go further.

SERVES 4–6

big bunch of dill, finely chopped

2 tbsp extra virgin olive oil

60g preserved lemons, finely chopped,
plus 1 tbsp of their preserving water

1 tsp caraway seeds

1 tsp coriander seeds, toasted and crushed

1 tsp caster sugar

1 tsp white wine vinegar

—

1. Combine all the ingredients in a bowl.

This is where the Top Five game gets painful, because I have one spot left and five absolutely essential herbs from which to choose. Should my allegiance lie with the year-round faithfuls or the summertime flings? If I said that sage brought up the rear – ready for butter and strings of spaghetti – to take up the fifth spot then I would still have neglected thyme (that multi-purpose, scented mountain herb), parsley (so abundant of all the soft herbs that it is almost a salad leaf), rosemary (those wild, intense needles) and bay (the herb that thinks it's a spice, which means I use it as both, and thus very often). Brava sauce puts three of these wonders to work.

BRAVA SAUCE

This is the sauce that accompanies the potatoes in patatas bravas, *the dish with spicy tomato sauce on fried potatoes named after the Spanish coastline where it originates. The Italian meaning of 'brava' (i.e. the feminine of bravo) seems equally fitting, because this immaculately choreographed dance between pimentón, chilli, wine, rosemary, bay and tomatoes is just delicious. Serve it on top of the* rosemary potatoes, alongside cheese, spicy sausage and a bottle of something big and red.

———

MAKES ENOUGH SAUCE FOR THE ROSEMARY POTATOES ON PAGES 159–160 (SERVES 4–6 PEOPLE)

5 tbsp extra virgin olive oil

2 garlic cloves, finely chopped

½ tsp dried chilli flakes

2 sprigs of thyme, leaves only

3 sprigs of rosemary, needles only, finely chopped

1 bay leaf

50ml red wine

1 x 400g tin of whole plum tomatoes

½ tsp sugar

½ tsp pimentón

———

1. Heat the oil in a saucepan over a medium heat and add the garlic, chilli, thyme, rosemary and bay leaf. Cook, stirring frequently so nothing sticks, for 2–3 minutes, until fragrant.

2. Add the wine, tinned tomatoes, sugar and pimentón and cook for 10 minutes before briefly removing the sauce from the heat and blitzing it with a hand blender.

3. Return to the heat and cook for a further 10–15 minutes until it has thickened and reduced enough to slop over potatoes like a very fragrant ketchup.

A nd here is a recipe that – like *salsa verde* – celebrates parsley. Though hard to grow outside in winter, I always have a packet of parsley in the fridge.

GREMOLATA

This is like a dry, and much-simplified, salsa verde and an enhanced seasoning for braised meats (it's traditionally served with the Milanese veal shin dish, osso buco), meaty stews or fish. You could also add it to simple pasta, like the store-cupboard recipe on pages 78–79. I usually make this in a mini blender but it's easy to make by hand.

____

SERVES 4

big bunch of flat-leaf parsley, leaves only, very finely chopped

grated zest of 2 unwaxed lemons

2 garlic cloves, very finely chopped

____

1. Combine the ingredients so you have consistent sprinkle of green, yellow and white. You have a gremolata.

After all that, the Top Five Herbs game always gets abandoned, each time ending with the conclusion that I just love them all. Arguably no dish celebrates herbs more than a tabbouleh. It's also a dish that welcomes improvisation, so perhaps a good recipe on which to close a chapter that encourages you to run and jump in the kitchen. Lastly, it's a dish I grew up eating and which I have carried forward into adult life, tweaking and tinkering with the recipe each time I make it – so perhaps the most apt recipe with which to conclude this book.

It would be easy to assume this to be a summer dish, which it is, but with a little resourcefulness you can swap seasonal vegetables in and out to reflect where you are in the year. Below is a base recipe to which you can introduce seasonal ingredients (peas and broad beans in spring; sweet baby plum tomatoes and cucumbers in summer; fig, finely sliced plums and some nuts in the autumn, more nuts and bitter leaves and small morsels of cauliflower or romanesco in winter). You want roughly 400g of these for the quantities below. On the herb front, try adding dill in spring and summer, tarragon in the autumn and finely chopped sage in winter. You could even play with the spices in the dressing . . .

TABBOULEH

My granny used to make tabbouleh, but hers was a very different beast from the one here. It is supposed to be a salad consisting predominantly of herbs, laced with just a little bulgur wheat to pad it out with coarseness.

—

SERVES 4

50g bulgur wheat

juice of 1 lemon

1 bunch of flat-leaf parsley

1 bunch of mint

2 large vine tomatoes or 10 baby plum tomatoes, finely diced

4 spring onions, finely chopped

4 tbsp cinnamon, lemon and garlic dressing (page 260)

Little Gem lettuce leaves, to serve

—

1. Rinse the bulgur wheat under cold running water several times, then transfer it to a bowl, add the lemon juice and let it soak in the juice for 10 minutes. Fluff with a fork and drain.

2. Wash, dry and finely chop the parsley leaves and stalks with a very sharp knife. It's really important to do this by hand – a blender will make it too pulpy. Do the same with the mint, and transfer the herbs to a large bowl.

3. Once you have chopped the tomatoes, drain off the excess juice and add them to the bowl with the herbs and finely chopped spring onions.

4. Sprinkle the bulgur wheat all over the salad, then pour the dressing over the bowlful.

5. Serve with some lettuce leaves dipped into the salad around the bowl's edge. These can be used to scoop it up.

Endnote

— . —

Our relationship with food says a lot about us. True to this book's subtitle, it 'makes us' – on many levels: what our mothers ate while we were growing inside them; how we are weaned; what we are fed as children – from liquidised mush to first solid morsels, and beyond; what we feed ourselves when we are first given licence to choose; whether we adhere to meal times; table etiquette (or not); whether or not we cook, and how we go about cooking if we do; where we buy our groceries; what ingredients we always have to hand; the language we use; our favourite things to eat; whether or not food is an agent of comfort . . . or of fear. Epigenetic research – the study of how environment and experience can determine, over generations, what 'switches on' the genes we inherit – is revealing how even the diets of our ancestors can have a bearing on how we turn out, not just physically, but mentally, emotionally and socially as well.

The premise of this book is that eating isn't merely a biological function, and that food has a more complex and less tangible role in our lives than plain sustenance. It's about posterity, survival, rituals, celebrations, grief, values, nature, obsessions, superstition, gender, memory, the list goes on. Most of all, food is surrounded by story. As human beings, food is something

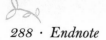

that we all share, but also experience independently – even uniquely. We all have our stories to tell, either about food, or in which food features, integrally or incidentally. I believe that telling these stories, sharing little details about ourselves, can both bring our differences to light *and* help us reach a place of understanding. Of seeing. Of feeling. (And – because it is food – hopefully of smelling and tasting too.)

This is not a reference book, nor is it one whose content is based on anything more than personal observation. In these pages I have tried to tap into the stories of my eight subjects – and some of my own – to expand on this idea of food transcending biology, to its role as an identifier and, even more abstractly, as an imaginative force. As I said, we connect through stories, so I hope that the stories told in these pages have inspired you to think about your own relationship with what you eat and how it identifies you.

Acknowledgements

I'd like to thank my publisher, Amanda Harris at Orion, for believing in this idea. To my original editor Tamsin English and, later on, Lucy Haenlein for all their hard work and support in getting this off the ground. Thanks to Mark McGinlay in publicity, Jessica Purdue in rights, Amy Davies in marketing, and to the design team - not least Loulou Clark for the beautiful cover art. And to Laura Nickoll for meticulously correcting my clumsiness with her brilliant copy editing. I am so lucky to have you as champions.

To my agent, Jon Elek, for making this happen! Also to Millie Hoskins and Amy Mitchell at United Agents.

To all the voices that appear in these pages – Anna Del Conte, Deborah Madison, Jamie Oliver, Susie Orbach, Yotam Ottolenghi, Claudia Roden, Stanley Tucci and Alice Waters. Also to Felicity Blunt, Margot Henderson and Rachel Roddy for their stories and inspiration.

To all my colleagues and columnists at the *Guardian* – thank you for the encouragement (and calories). Special thanks to all those who have allowed me to use their recipes.

To all my early readers, mostly to my mum Caroline Holland, and also to Mary Myers, Katharine Rosser, Sophie Andrews, Dale Berning Sawa, Jessica Hopkins, and Rosie Birkett. Your thoughts and suggestions have been invaluable.

To my family, friends and feeders. To my mum and dad for everything in that blue tin box and beyond; to Louise Webb for her support (and for bringing up a boy who can cook), and to Freddie for the food memories we've already made, and those that are still to come. Love you all.

Index